Praise for

"There is no hope for great sex (or a great life, actually) when we are filled with shame. Rena Martine has written a gorgeous, pink-carpeted pathway out of the shame, guilt, and self-doubt that restricts and shuts down our aliveness. Open these pages and step into the expansion you have longed for!"

—**Regena (Mama gena) Thomashauer**, *New York Times* bestselling author of *Pussy: A Reclamation,* founder of The School of Womanly Arts

"Using her own personal experience and the stories of her countless coaching clients, Rena Martine provides an authentic, accessible, and reassuring road map to help free you from sexual shame. Wherever you are in the journey of embracing a pleasurable and shame-free sexual style that works for you, this book will guide and empower you! Chock-full of wisdom and thought-provoking exercises, this book should be required reading for every sexual being!"

—**Laurie Mintz**, author of *Becoming Cliterate: Why Orgasm Equality Matters—And How To Get It*

"Rena Martine didn't just write a powerful book, she created a new genre—Sex Betterment. *The Sex You Want* isn't just about sexuality and how to have the kind of sex you've always wanted but about building a better life and relationship with the self. This needs to be on every nightstand, especially men's."

—**John Kim**, LMFT (The Angry Therapist), author of *Single. On Purpose.*

"The best sex you can possibly have starts with authenticity, and Rena Martine proves it. *The Sex You Want* includes hands-on practices to rinse out any shame you've got about sex and replaces it with a life that reflects the sexual person you already are."

—**Emily Morse**, founder + host of *Sex With Emily*

"What a treasure to have a sex-positive, educationally accurate and clinically effective book for those seeking pleasure, permission and true empowerment. Rena Martine's journey into sexual liberation is a must-read for anyone taking their first steps toward a more passionate life."

—**Holly Richmond**, PhD, certified sex therapist and author of *Reclaiming Pleasure: A Sex-Positive Guide for Moving Past Sexual Trauma and Living a Passionate Life*

"Every woman needs to read this book. Rena's approach to sexual healing is direct, profound, and expansive. I learned new ways to honor my sexual past that leave me feeling lighter, connected, and confidently sensual."

—**Nadège**, sex scholar, bestselling author, and founder of Pleasure Science

"On my own path, I've found that romantic liberation is anything but linear. The good news is that means we never stop growing. The exercises in this book generously help readers navigate the labyrinth that is attempting to live a freer, sexier, more joyful life."

—**Rachel Krantz**, author of *Open: An Uncensored Memoir of Love, Liberation, and Non-Monogamy*

"Martine weaves personal anecdotes and solid education to create a guidebook for anyone looking to expand their sexual horizons. *The Sex You Want* is the perfect book for anyone who is feeling like their sex life is missing that special something and are looking for real life, real human examples for how to take it to the next level."

—**Allison Moon**, author of *Getting It*

THE SEX YOU WANT

A SHAMELESS JOURNEY to DEEP INTIMACY, HONEST PLEASURE, and a LIFE YOU LOVE

RENA MARTINE

For Jaydee

Copyright © 2024 by Rena Martine
Cover and internal design © 2024 by Sourcebooks
Cover design by Sara Wood
Internal design by Tara Jaggers/Sourcebooks

Sourcebooks and the colophon are registered trademarks of Sourcebooks.

This publication is designed to provide accurate and authoritative information in regard to the subject matter covered. It is sold with the understanding that the publisher is not engaged in rendering legal, accounting, or other professional service. If legal advice or other expert assistance is required, the services of a competent professional person should be sought. —*From a Declaration of Principles Jointly Adopted by a Committee of the American Bar Association and a Committee of Publishers and Associations*

All brand names and product names used in this book are trademarks, registered trademarks, or trade names of their respective holders. Sourcebooks is not associated with any product or vendor in this book.

Published by Sourcebooks
P.O. Box 4410, Naperville, Illinois 60567-4410
(630) 961-3900
sourcebooks.com

Cataloging-in-Publication Data is on file with the Library of Congress.

Printed and bound in Canada.
MBP 10 9 8 7 6 5 4 3 2 1

The book of love is long and boring
No one can lift the damn thing
It's full of charts and facts and figures
And instructions for dancing

But I, I love it when you read to me
And you, you can read me anything

"THE BOOK OF LOVE,"
THE MAGNETIC FIELDS

Contents

Part 3: Make Sex Fun Again

Prologue: The Beginning of a Happy Ending

'm about to pay for sex.

I've sent child molesters and rapists to prison for life. I've been called to crime scenes with brains and organs spilled onto sidewalks. I've donned head-to-toe surgical gear during autopsies to protect me from the smell of death.

But I've never hired a sex worker.

Much less a dominatrix.

I've also never played submissive to a woman. Never met someone for the explicit purpose of having sex while stone-cold sober in the middle of the afternoon. Never had a woman bring me to orgasm. But judging from her suggestion that I bring "any toys you want me to use on you," I have a feeling she's planning to change all that today.

I pull up to the "dungeon," which is actually a midsize suburban home in the deep valley of Los Angeles. I park on the street out front and take a deep breath. This is a first for me, not only because I'm paying for (what I hope will be) a happy ending but because I'm allowing someone into the deep recesses of my sexual imagination. A place that used to be shameful.

I'm greeted by Mistress Moxie—the name given to me by the

dominatrix I've hired—at the door. She's a petite blond wearing an off-the-shoulder sweater and a pair of leggings. Moxie has the look of a young suburban mom who has gotten dolled up to take a trip to the local mall, not an intimidating sex worker who is used to inflicting pain on (primarily male) clients.

She escorts me into the bedroom in the back, which I recognize as the largest of the playrooms featured on the dungeon's website.

"This is your first time, right?" she asks.

I giggle nervously before answering, "Yes."

Maybe because of all the situations my professional life has landed me in, the wide variety of pain implements hanging from the wall to my left reminds me of just how much trust I am putting in a total stranger. But I remember: my job as a prosecutor was to peer into the depravity of what humans are capable of, and her job is to fulfill my sexual fantasies.

The reason I'm here on a random Saturday in December? I've just turned forty, and I want to commemorate my sexual liberation in a noteworthy way. Bigger than the sex parties I now attend. A punctuation in the intense role-play my partner and I indulge in where I am submissive to him as his "baby girl." I want to have an experience with a mommy to complement what he provides me as my Daddy.

And I'm about to pay $350 for it.

We go over a few formalities: my request for no pain, whether I'm okay with anal play, and the "tribute" (i.e., payment). Then, with her guidance, we begin setting the stage.

"Okay, so I'm thinking you'll be lying down on the bed when I come in," she suggests. "Do you want to take your dress off now? Or do you want me to unbutton it as part of the scene?"

"I'm wearing lingerie underneath this. So it could be fun for you to unbutton the dress yourself?" I don't actually know what the fuck I'm doing. But I remind myself: life exists just outside one's comfort zone.

Plus, Moxie *does* know what she's doing, and she nods. "Sounds good. So why don't you just lie down on the bed. I'm going to leave for a few minutes and change into something sexier."

I do as I'm told. And as I'm in repose on the four-poster bed looking down at my light-pink thigh-highs and black baby-doll shoes, I can hear Moxie and some of the other dominatrices chatting beyond the closed door.

"Wait—are we all still going out for drinks tonight?"

"Oh my god! He hasn't texted you back yet?"

I shut my eyes and imagine I'm somewhere else. Not because I *want* to be somewhere else but because I could be almost *anywhere else* in that moment and this background chatter would be completely normal. But in this context, it's pretty hilarious.

Moxie returns in character, wearing a black lace bustier, garter, and stockings. She purses her lips and grazes her finger seductively down her cleavage. "Your daddy told me you two have been playing together. Don't be scared. I'm not mad. I told him I wanted to have my way with you. I'm going to train you to be a very good girl for him."

This is exactly what I was hoping for: a mere extension from my role-play at home, not some separate and distinct scenario where I would have to build my fantasy from the ground up. She definitely understood the assignment.

Moxie unbuttons my dress and chains my wrists to the corners of the bed.

And as I'm lying there, offering myself up to be imprisoned, it strikes me how far I've come. Because tomorrow, I'll be speaking in front of an organization of one hundred female lawyers: women who knew me as a respected attorney. Women who may not recognize the pink-haired, tattooed person who will stand before them. The exact type of women who probably need my guidance the most. I start ruminating on how I'll break the ice:

My name is Rena, and I spent fourteen years as a Deputy District Attorney with the LA County DA's Office, where I specialized in cases of sex crimes, child abuse, and domestic violence. And I'm here today to give you permission to fall out of love with what you thought you wanted.

"I've been wondering what your pretty little nipples and pussy look like," Moxie whispers in my ear, snapping me back into the moment. My mind is focused. "Now it's time to get you nice and wet." She slides a gloved finger inside me, and glancing at the assortment of sex toys on the bed—some hers, some mine— she grabs a large black vibrating wand, which happens to be my favorite. It's like the KitchenAid of sex toys: sturdy, reliable, and amazing at its job. A true sexual workhorse.

But this toy—like a lot of new vibrating sex toys—has about twenty different vibration patterns. And in the throes of Moxie trying to grab the toy with her lubed-up, latex-gloved hands, she's switched the setting to one of those annoying patterns that seem more like a novelty than anything designed to actually get you off. And then my sweet and sensual mommy breaks character.

"Fuck. Okay. I can't get it back to the other setting," she mumbles while trying to keep the wand from tumbling out of her slick hands.

I—lying on my back, arms totally outstretched, wrists chained to the bedposts—have no idea what to do. "I mean, I wish I could help you, but…"

We make eye contact and both start laughing. And in that moment, I'm reminded that we're nothing more than two imperfect women in a room playing make-believe. But instead of being a young girl pretending to be a beautiful princess or a schoolteacher, I am in fact a forty-year-old woman sprawled naked on a bed pretending to be an innocent girl.

The truth is I've been reconciling contradictions most of my adult life. And while I don't plan on sharing today's particular details with the crowd I'll be addressing tomorrow, I mentally sketch out what I *do* plan on sharing:

When the highs were high—when justice was served—it was the best job in the world. But the lows were indescribable. I reached my breaking point prosecuting sex crimes when I realized the system was broken. I reached the breaking point in my marriage when I realized I didn't want the white picket fence of conventional monogamy. And I reached my breaking point as a lawyer when I could no longer derive any meaning from it.

And then Moxie gets *me* to a breaking point. After using sex toys in all my orifices and bringing me to orgasm twice, she asks, "Was there anything else you were hoping to try?"

The answer is a resounding no. I'm fully and completely satisfied.

And I realize I want these attorneys, this group of one hundred women who I'm speaking to tomorrow, to ask themselves the same question—*Was there anything else you were hoping to try?*—about their careers, their relationships, their life purpose.

Instead, I decide I'll end my speech with a question that opens the door to all those other curiosities, which I've posed to thousands of women—clients, students, listeners—since becoming an intimacy coach:

What would your life look like if shame weren't an option?

The aftermath in Moxie's room is *my* answer to that question. Puppy pads littering the bed, absorbing my bodily fluids. A wreckage of vibrators and dildos left after a sexual tornado. And me, struggling to find the thong Moxie had slipped off me an hour earlier.

Finally dressed (and already worrying about traffic on the way home), we begin our goodbyes.

"This was a lot of fun. I'm game to do it again, any time!" she says, hugging me on the way out.

I'm not a john cowering out of a brothel. I hold my head up high, the winter LA sun kissing my smiling face. Because this isn't a walk of shame, a walk I know all too well. This is a walk of pride. Shameless is my badge of honor.

Introduction

B ack in 2012, some friends convinced me to sign up on a mainstream dating app. I went on dates with thirty different men. And on first dates with said men, I asked them all—yep, even the ones I knew I didn't want to see again—the same question: *What are your views on monogamy?*

I was met with responses like "I'm pretty traditional when it comes to that," "nonmonogamy just makes things too complicated," and "I'm a one-woman kind of guy."

As people do in polite conversation, they'd then flip the question on me. And my typical, murky response usually came out like, "The idea of having something other than monogamy has always appealed to me."

I often say that curiosity is the antidote to judgment, and there was an utter lack of curiosity on their parts. The conversations stopped there. My inner turmoil persisted.

But I couldn't beat them, so I joined them. I married #30.

And in the six years we were together, I never sought out infidelity. I wasn't on dating apps or sneaking behind my husband's back. But it found me. It's like telling a masseuse you don't need her to focus on a specific area, then feeling her massage a knot in your shoulder you hadn't realized was there: sometimes it takes another person's touch to unlock the pain you've been carrying with you.

And the pain I was carrying was the complete loss of eroticism in my relationship. I felt like a sister. A best friend. A roommate. A travel buddy. I didn't feel like a lover or sexual being.

These weren't affairs. I didn't want something long, drawn out, and stable. I wanted something short, passionate, finite. I wasn't looking to jump ship; I was looking to swim.

And about five years in, I realized I was drowning.

"I can't stop cheating on my husband," I told my new therapist during our first session, "and you need to fix me."

I assumed there was something pathological about me. That I wouldn't want to be a member of any club that would have someone like me as a member. That I didn't feel worthy of love, which was why I would shut down sexually and emotionally once someone truly committed to me. I assumed that was why I couldn't be monogamous. So I came to her like a possessed soul would come to a priest, begging her to exorcise my shame demons.

And week after week, she convinced me there was nothing to expel. I wasn't *bad*. My yearning for an unconventional relationship structure wasn't some sort of inherent flaw to be drawn out of me. "You deserve to be happy, Rena. You're allowed to be you."

And as I sat across from her one Monday night, she said, earnestly, "There's a scream buried deep inside you, and it's dying to get out."

Those words—words that I will carry with me until the day I die—ended up being the combination to unlock my freedom.

The next morning, I told my husband I wanted a divorce.

The next few years ended up being the most transformative

period of my personal life. I traveled to Denmark and Mexico alone. I started googling sex clubs in my city (and later realized the best clubs aren't found on Google). I bought myself lingerie. I read Esther Perel and Emily Nagoski. I didn't miss an episode of Dan Savage's *Savage Lovecast*. I started sleeping with women again for the first time since college. I tried things I thought I'd love but didn't (costumed role-play) and loved things I'd already written off as "not my thing" (anal sex).

I began indulging in a lifetime's worth of sexual curiosities. And in that journey, I partnered with a man who enjoys coloring outside the lines as much as I do.

Yes, I had dropped a bomb in my life.

But I was building my dream home from the ashes.

Still, my house was only half-finished. Because as I was designing a life of my choosing, I started to see that the longest committed relationship I'd ever had—my career as a DA—was dying a slow death. Like a companionate couple who stays together until the kids turn eighteen, my plan was to ride this relationship out until the age of fifty when I could collect a pension. In the meantime, I'd go back to school part-time and begin working toward licensure to become a therapist. If I could change one woman's life the way my therapist had changed mine, I reasoned, I would feel like I'd had a fulfilling career.

And then the pandemic hit.

After I'd baked all the bread and binged all the TV, I faced my existential reckoning. None of us knew how long this would last. Did I want to spend the six-plus years (and a few hundred thousand dollars in college loans) it would take to become a therapist? Or was there a way I could start helping people *now*?

I enrolled in a coaching certification program. Just as I knew when I entered law school that I was there to become a DA and not just a lawyer, I also knew I didn't want to be a generic life coach. I wanted to be a women's intimacy coach.

I asked myself: *What would I have needed at the beginning of my journey to work through my sexual shame? Is there a way I could have bypassed those years of therapy, books, podcasts, tears, anguish, and feelings of being alone—alone, broken, and dysfunctional? Can I help women in committed relationships salvage what they have in a way I wasn't able to? Can I show single women they deserve more and prevent them from getting into unsatisfying relationships in the first place?*

From there, my signature Shameless coaching program was born. Clients began knocking on my virtual door. I spent my lunch hours and evenings in sessions, all the while resenting the unsatisfying work I was performing at the DA's Office. Yet another scream, dying to be let out.

So I dropped another bomb. But this one was bigger and could be nuclear. Jumping from a civil service job with fantastic benefits to becoming an entrepreneur without a predictable income was the scariest decision I've ever made.

And it's been the most rewarding.

Since leaving the DA's Office, I've worked with thousands of women as both an educator and a coach by helping them love their bodies, experience deep intimacy, and have great sex, shame-free.

They've spanned the globe: from Hawaii to Alabama, from Germany to Tasmania. I've worked with women from their early twenties to their sixties. Cis women and trans women. Celebs and stay-at-home moms. Therapists and doctors. Strippers and schoolteachers. Queer women and straight women and women at every point in between. If you are a living and breathing woman who knows you're missing something out there—deeper intimacy, honest pleasure, a life you *love*—this book is for you. Because shame doesn't care what your background is or how much money you make. It doesn't care what color your skin is or whether you went to college.

But here's what I've also learned: if you *can* become shameless when it comes to sex—often the most hidden part of who you are—it will spill into *every facet of your life*.

My own journey to shame-free intimacy had felt like a full-time job. And education isn't the same as *guidance*. None of my books, podcasts, or even my therapist could tell me how to find sex clubs or that the type of BDSM dynamic I was looking for was actually called DD/LG. There weren't any dating guides espousing the virtue of *not* waiting to have sex or saying that it's okay to need a vibrator to orgasm.

And there weren't real faces. No one to reassure me with "Oh, I've been there, woman. Here's how you navigate this." Therapists can't reveal their personal stories. Most sexual self-help books are written from an academic or clinical perspective. I wanted to feel normal by actually hearing from people *like me* rather than relying on anonymous content creators, professional sex workers, or case study avatars.

This is the book I wish I'd had during my own journey. It's composed of lessons told through stories: my own and those of the clients and students I've had the honor of serving. And no subject is off-limits. Threesomes. Hiring a dominatrix. BDSM. Sex parties. This isn't your mother's guide to good sex and relationships.

I've changed names and small details *only* to the extent they're necessary to protect a person's identity. A lot of self-help authors will resort to creating avatars or amalgamations of real people to get their point across. I'm not doing that. My recounting of client stories and exact quotes is based on copious session notes, email/text exchanges, and my (human and therefore imperfect) recollection of our work together.

Because what my own journey has taught me (and what the success of Shameless has confirmed) is that one of the best ways to normalize our experiences as women is through the stories of other real women, not imaginary people who've been concocted to fit a lesson plan. My goal in this book is to make you feel like you're having a conversation with friends over a (reasonably priced) bottle of wine, not being lectured to from an ivory tower or enlightened by a spiritual guru.

Yes, I will also educate you. Not as someone who has a PhD in sexuality (I don't). There are plenty of ample resources out there to provide you the comprehensive sex education you were likely deprived of (and I'm going to point you toward some of them!). As someone who's sifted through a lot of that information, I'm going to give you the remaining golden nuggets: the research and data that have helped me and my clients the most. Because the fact that 96 percent of women have fantasized about BDSM can help you make sense of your sexual fantasies. And knowing that—year by year—more women are cheating on their spouses might help you think about why it's important to make sexual novelty a priority *now*.

But knowledge isn't power; action is power. Which is why I'm going to tell you *how* to do the damned thing. I'll be giving you straightforward steps to help you love your body, experience deep intimacy, and have great sex, shame-free. Some of these (especially in the first section of the book) will come in the form of homework assignments and mindset practices. Other suggestions will come in the form of conversation starters and practical action steps.

I'll also point you toward some products, companies, and organizations I vouch for. In our fast-moving world, by the time you're reading this book, there may be better options out there! I'm willing to take this risk to give you as much concrete guidance as I can. In exchange, I'll ask you to give me some grace if you're tempted to roll your eyes at anything outdated here. Deal?

You'll get a lot more out of this book if you have a dedicated place to take notes and complete the assignments. Grab a journal or create a document on your computer. If you can stay organized with your work, I promise you'll walk away with one hell of a wellness tool kit.

But before we jump in, I need you to promise me something: *Don't yuck anyone's yum.* Chances are you'll come across some stories (and if you've made it this far, you probably already have) that don't sit well with you. But one person's yuck is another person's yum. I personally dislike oysters: I've tried them, and they're not my jam. It wasn't until I asked a friend to describe what *she* likes about oysters—the buttery texture, the way they slide down your throat—that I understood the appeal. Curiosity is the antidote to judgment.

Let's get curious.

PART 1

FREE YOUR MIND

1

Start Visualizing

"There were old guys. And snacks."

I'd asked my dear friend to come over and tell me all about the sex party she'd gone to. This wasn't the recap I was expecting.

As we sat across from each other, sipping Trader Joe's rosé in my backyard, I demanded more: "Start from the beginning. Don't leave out a single detail."

You see, I'd never known (or at least I hadn't *known* I'd known) anyone who'd been to a play party before. But my curiosity wasn't that of a voyeur; I wasn't looking to get turned on by the story. This was emotional masochism: I was holding up my wounded soul, passing her the salt, and telling her to rub it in...*harder*.

My then husband joined us at the table, nodding, laughing at the appropriate times. Hell, even chiming in ("So what kind of snacks were there, exactly?"). And with each clarifying question I asked, I wondered if he could smell it on me: the desperate longing for a life that was nothing like the one we'd built.

As she started recounting the details—a guy flashing his penis at the female partygoers through a long silk robe, a threesome of strangers positioned into an Eiffel Tower, she and her date locking themselves in the bathroom to escape the untoward advances of lecherous men—I felt pure, unadulterated *envy*.

Don't get me wrong: the party sounded terrible. I pined for the *option* of going to a shitty sex party rather than going to no party at all.

The end of my marriage a year later gave me a chance. A chance to make good on what I'd missed out on. A chance to create my own sketch instead of filling in someone else's paint by number. A chance to go to a sex club.

I'd learned about the club through Tina, a friend of a friend who knew infinitely more about play parties than I did (which, at the time, wasn't saying much). After getting a "Sure, why not?" green light from my current partner, I'd applied online and quickly received approval for our couple's membership.

As our Uber approached a seemingly abandoned building in a desolate part of East LA close to midnight on a Friday, I thought of crime scenes I'd responded to mere blocks away. This wasn't a kind part of town.

After checking in with security, we were ushered into a massive room: a loud dance floor glistened to our right. An all-you-can-eat Indian buffet (yes, seriously) lined the wall to our left. A woman stood guard behind a bar in the back, ready to protect our BYOBs.

But there wasn't another soul in sight.

I know I said I'd be okay with a shitty sex party, but this felt like a scene from a David Lynch movie.

As we soon discovered, the inhabitants of this ghastly soiree had all retreated downstairs to a large space that looked like an architectural spider: a boxing ring–sized mattress in its center and tiny bedrooms splintering outward like bizarre appendages.

The lighting was low: bright enough to see women's heads bobbing up and down over men's crotches but dim enough that I wouldn't be able to pick anyone's face out of a lineup.

"I need a drink."

Bourbons in hand, we eventually made our way to a covered outdoor patio where a handful of (fully clothed) couples gathered around a decorative fire pit. Relieved to find a semblance of normalcy in this surreal, not-so-fun fun house, I nestled in and got straight to the point: "So...what are you all doing here?"

A couple in their sixties had been coming weekly—"Sometimes Friday *and* Saturday!"—for a few years.

"It's really saved our marriage," they said. And I believed them.

A thirtysomething pair had trekked from the next county over while a family member babysat their kids. The husband worked in insurance. The wife carried a knockoff Louis Vuitton bag. They seemed nice. Suburban. Normal.

My partner and I made our way downstairs and got down to business on the spider's huge mattress of a belly. We started having the type of rough sex we dabbled in at home: me play fighting, him overpowering and having his way with me.

It was all sexy fun and games until I said the word "stop" within earshot of another couple. In our case, that was code for "keep going." But to them, it meant something like "this woman is being sexually assaulted and we need to help her."

After some awkward reassurances ("I was just pretending!"),

we finished up in one of the private side rooms, eventually making our way out of the party, the lingering smell of Indian curry bidding us farewell.

As I recounted the night's antics, awkwardness and all, to friends at a bridal shower the next day, I was beaming. Because after all, I'd been to a shitty sex party. Which was still better than no sex party at all.

While I was training to become a coach, I suspected there were other women out there like me: women who had their own core desires that were waiting to be unlocked. Women who needed someone to bring them the key and gently nudge them by saying, "Why don't you try this?"

What I hadn't anticipated, though, was how deep some of these desires had been buried, how unknown they were. I knew even before my divorce that I really wanted to go to a sex party. But not all my clients had a similar conviction or clarity around what it is they truly *crave*. I had to figure out a way to elicit it from them.

I remembered an assignment I'd gotten once upon a time in a business coaching program: write down 101 things I wanted to do, be, or accomplish in life.

My first ten things included items like these:

- Travel a lot.
- Own a vacation home.
- Be my own boss.

But when I got to ten, I felt stuck. "Well, that's it. I'm boring. What else can I cover?"

Instead of throwing in the towel, though, I pushed myself to expand. To imagine. To get *really* specific.

- I want to see a penguin in the wild.
- I want to take a pasta-making class in Italy.
- I want to have a weekend cabin in Idyllwild.

And then I couldn't stop. I hit 101 a lot quicker than I thought I could and actually had to cut myself off from writing more.

This exercise had been profound for me. I saw themes emerge. (Turns out about a dozen involved cute wild animals, and very few involved owning material things. This told me a *lot* about my values!) I saw desires unlock. Once I was tasked with coming up with a huge list of my dreams, my dreams expanded to fill the list.

Wanting my clients to have similar revelations, I adapted the exercise by cutting the list down from 101 to 27 (I've found that 27 items strikes a perfect balance between encouraging expansion while minimizing burnout) and making it specific to intimacy.

Screech. Let me stop there for a second.

In the context of this book, I'm not using the term *intimacy* as some polite euphemism for "sex." Intimacy is being truly seen (and, by definition, *allowing yourself to be seen*) by another person, whether that be emotionally or sexually, platonically or romantically. Because there are people out there who can have sex with a stranger they never talk to again but struggle to give their best friend a hug.

But intimacy also means allowing yourself to be seen in *the world around you*. Saying "fuck it" and wearing the bikini anyway? Intimacy. Sticking to your boundaries at work? Also intimacy.

This intimacy bucket list serves as the jumping-off point for every single Shameless client, and it's proven to be invaluable. And much like the 101 things exercise I'd completed, it reveals a ton about a person's values.

When client Sasha and I started working together, for example, she had a few overarching goals: "I want sex to be fun and playful. I want to feel sexy." Those goals are the intimacy equivalent of "I want to travel a lot": generic and immeasurable.

Sasha is a science researcher by day. In her free time, she runs marathons and hikes in exotic travel destinations. She wears her hair air-dried and has a penchant for Patagonia outerwear and baseball caps.

As someone who doesn't fit into any of the above categories, I knew I could make zero assumptions about what "fun," "sexy," and "playful" meant to her. So we started digging into her list of 27 Things, and a few jumped out immediately:

- Role-play.
- Live out a fantasy.
- Have an alter ego for play.

And when it came time for Sasha to write an erotic short story as one of her first homework assignments, this theme tracked:

It's Friday night, and Lilian (my alter ego) finds herself throwing back gin and tonics after a hard work week. She's at a Latin bar with a mix of music playing in the background: reggaeton, bachata, salsa. She's waiting for her date, Moises, to arrive. They had been on two dates prior, meeting for casual coffee and the other for a casual dinner. Tonight was the first meeting at a bar, so she was nervous. Lilian was new to the dating scene and never dated much. She always found herself in long-term relationships that never seemed to work out. Freshly single, she was giving the dating apps a try.

She went into steamy details, ending with her surrendering to Moises (and his mouth) back at his place.

The assignment had called for a 200- to 500-word story; Sasha's was 1,228. Sasha may not have known how to be sexy, but Lilian did.

"What if you took yourself out for drinks this week...as Lilian?" I suggested. With zero hesitation whatsoever (marathon runner!), she accepted the challenge and agreed to send me a photo for accountability.

And that photo blew me away. Sasha's curly black hair had been replaced with a sleek, side-banged auburn wig. Smoky eyes. Red lips. A light-pink cocktail in a coupe glass instead of the beer Sasha normally drank.

As we continued working together, Sasha began filling in the details of Lilian's persona.

"What do you think Lilian likes to wear under her clothes?" I asked.

"Lingerie," she said. "But I've never owned any."

I encouraged Sasha to order a few pieces from a site with a generous return policy. "You don't have to keep anything, but try to push outside your comfort zone. Take some photos. Have fun!"

Challenge accepted, yet again.

Two lingerie sets arrived at her doorstep. "They fit perfectly! I'd never bought anything to make me feel sexy. Why didn't I do this sooner?"

She kept both and later ordered a kimono and patterned blindfold to breathe some more life into Lilian.

To my immense pride, Sasha also posted Lilian's photo on Instagram with the caption, "Well hello there alter ego...where have you been hiding for so long? When did we start taking life so seriously and stop having fun?"

Exactly, woman.

Sasha's list of 27 Things was the foundation for the work we did together. And it's going to be your foundation too!

Your 27 Things

Create a list of 27 Things you want to *do* or *feel* in your intimate life that you haven't up until now. The items on your list don't need to be attainable tomorrow or even in the next five years. You probably don't want to go to a shitty sex party. And maybe the idea of having an alter ego isn't your jam. My job isn't to tell you what's on your bucket list. Your bucket. Your list.

These can be emotions (toward yourself or another person) or actions (sexual or nonsexual) that you'd like to experience. Think of this as a set of intimacy life goals, one that looks into an indefinite future.

You may get to five or even ten and be tempted to do what I almost did: wave the white flag and declare yourself boring as fuck. Remember, part of the process here is pushing past the resistance.

Here's a smattering of goals from past Shameless clients. I know it might be tempting to pick and choose from the list and shortcut your way up to twenty-seven. Try your best to use the list to get your wheels turning, not to drive you to the end.

- Have sex under the stars.
- Dance more.
- Read sex scenes in books to my husband.
- Wear a bikini to the beach without a cover-up.
- Have a one-night stand.
- Have sex standing up, bent over with one leg in the air.
- Tell someone I love them without needing to hear it back.
- Film myself having sex with a partner.
- Learn and experience tantric sex.
- Release shame from having herpes.
- Feel what it's like to orgasm through self-pleasure.
- Be open to falling in love again.
- Turn up to a man's house in just lingerie and a coat.
- Adopt a pet together.
- Orgasm control with a partner that actually feels safe and hot and works!
- Play with food: desserts, strawberries, ice cream, chocolate, etc.
- Not feel shame around hormonal excess hair/growth and lower tummy fluffiness.
- Be able to implement my vibrator in the bedroom comfortably.
- Go to a nude beach.
- Be able to give someone an authentic hug if they are feeling sad.
- Stay interested in sex once I actually get to know someone.
- Get out of the passenger seat of my life and drive!

- Get pushed by my partner on that iconic photo swing in Bali.
- Experience multiple romantic relationships.
- Try anal sex.
- Be okay with looking at myself in a full-length mirror.
- Go to a burlesque show.
- Peg a guy.
- Stop bringing so much anxiety to my relationship.
- Be a bi-curious woman's first female experience.
- Be clear about my boundaries.

As you can see, some of these are specific and measurable (you could take a photo of it to prove you'd done it). Some are a bit more amorphous and intangible. As often as you can, opt for the former to make it easier to track your progress.

Once you've got your list, take a look through it, and pick *one* goal you can take *one* small step toward achieving this week. Want to go to a burlesque show? Look online to find one in your area. Curious to try anal? Buy some lube and a set of butt plugs. Want to feel okay looking at yourself in a full-length mirror? Spend a minute every day looking at just your face in the mirror, then gradually work your way down. Can't book a ticket to Bali this week? (Life's rough, huh?) Find a local spot and get your partner (or a friend or your phone's self-timer) to snap some fun shots of you.

Baby steps are key here. You'll notice Sasha's assignment wasn't to create a dating profile as Lilian and have wild, passionate sex with a stranger or to stock her drawer full of designer lingerie. While I'm all in favor in jumping in and doing the damned thing, if you do it too quickly, you run the risk of your brain freaking the fuck out ("Mayday! This is not safe!") and ditching the whole idea to begin with.

So ask yourself: what's the babiest (questionable whether this is an actual word, but get used to seeing it!) step I can take toward crossing one of these off my list? And do that thing.

In addition to concrete action steps, your 27 Things list will help you understand what your core sexual values are so you can gauge compatibility with current or prospective partners down the road (you'll learn more about how to do that in Lesson 12, "Do It Soon"). Think of core sexual values like the GPS of your sex life: they help you navigate your sexual experiences and preferences. These values can include beliefs about sexual orientation, gender identity, and consent.

Your list is a compass that directs you to your true north. Come back to it, time and time again. It'll show you where you've been and guide you to the next stop on your journey!

Rewrite Your Story

saw a lot of porn as a kid. There was a rotating library of *Playboy*, *Hustler*, and *Penthouse* magazines next to the toilet in my parents' bathroom. My dad kept a locked filing cabinet full of VHSs in his office that (unbeknownst to him) I regularly hacked into with a bent paper clip.

Most of the women I know now grew up pretty sheltered when it comes to sex: "One time, I heard my parents doing it, and I swear it scarred me for life!"

Not me. I heard my parents doing it. Talking about it. Talking about how one of my uncles doesn't like going down on my aunt and how pissed off it makes her. I know that my mom's ob-gyn suggested my dad start wearing looser pants (it was the late 1970s) and recommended they cut down on sex from three times a day to once a day to increase my mom's chances of getting pregnant. I know I was conceived during a quickie before guests arrived at a party my parents were hosting.

There isn't a right or wrong here. For every family hoping to not fuck up their kid by hiding sex, there is a family like mine that treats it like any other topic of conversation. As far as they're concerned, there's no T or M in TMI. It's all just information. Now that we're adults, it makes for fun holidays and interesting family text threads, full of double entendres and inappropriate memes.

Which is why the story I'm about to tell you is so surprising.

Because of my early exposure to porn, I knew more about the mechanics of sex than the average teenage girl. But I knew very little about the emotions of sex. I hadn't thought of sex as sacred; it was precisely the opposite. Sex was crass. Sex was vulgar. Men wanted it *all the time*. And if you want men to like you, you'd better start by being good at it.

In my five four, slightly chubby frame, I didn't look like the women I'd seen on screen. But wasn't there a way I could make up for that? I'd watched enough porn at this point to think I knew how to give a blow job. And I assumed boys would like me for it.

It turns out they did...but the girls at my high school didn't share the sentiment. And as I waited for my mom to pick me up from school on a fall day in my freshman year, a few older girls (who happened to be close with some of the guys on the receiving ends of said blow jobs) cornered me, got in my face, and called me a slut.

"Who are those girls, and what's their problem?" my mom asked as I hopped into the family Suburban.

"Oh, nothing. Can you drop me off at my friend's house? We're gonna go shopping for homecoming dresses."

Once when I was at my friend's house, a page on my beeper (yep, this was the 1990s and pre cell phones) came through. I called my mom, who explained she was coming back to get me. "We'll talk about it when I pick you up."

But I knew. Of course she'd driven back to the school and asked the girls what their fucking problem was. Of course she had. My mother got into trouble regularly in high school for fighting with the other girls—girls who were jealous of her because all their boyfriends wanted her. She proudly recounted stories of teasing her hair up really big and hiding razor blades in it, "So those bitches would cut their hands if they went to pull my hair."

To this day, I get nauseous thinking about the conversation my parents sat me down for once I got home. A conversation that could've gone something like, "Rena, what's going on? It's natural to want to explore sexually. Are you being safe? Are they being respectful to you?"

Instead, I was asked to give them a list of every guy I had ever given a blow job to. I lied and said it was only three.

"None of them even go to my high school." Also a lie.

This was the first and only conversation (if you can call it that) we ever had about the birds and the bees. Even though my family joked a lot about sex, I didn't learn a single thing from my parents about how to be sexual. I learned that sex was completely normal, but because I was shamed for wanting it, *I* must be abnormal.

Gone were the days of my bedroom door being closed when I had friends over or the days of boys being allowed to pick me up from my house. All my parents saw was a daughter who'd become a slut. A zombie who walked the earth preying on teenage dick instead of brains.

"Rena...you understand that's neglect, right?" my therapist

asked me years later as I recounted all the sexual imagery I was exposed to as a child.

As a prosecutor, I'd handled cases where children were being tortured and beaten by their mothers. An infant who'd been sodomized to death. A boy left in his stroller on the sidewalk during winter wearing nothing but a diaper, abandoned by his meth-addicted father.

So no. I didn't see leaving porn lying around as a form of neglect. It's not like my parents were showing it to me. It was just...there.

"Your little brain didn't understand how to process what you were seeing. It only makes sense why sex is wrapped up in so much shame for you. Why you've now shut that part of you off. How could it not be?"

I now know that so much of my adult understandings—of sex, of sex appeal, of intimacy, of beauty—was implanted into me. By porn. By my family. By what I saw in the media. It hadn't been my own.

Decades later, I've written a new story for myself. One where sex is a form of play and fun. Where it's something that can be done slowly and passionately...or hungrily, like animals in heat. Where women don't have to look like porn stars to be sexy. Where we can be smart and sexy at the same time. Where giving blow jobs isn't a way to get guys to like us but something we choose to do (or not do) depending on the mood we're in. Where there's no lying. No cheating. No double standards. Where sex is something we can revere *and* joke about. Where there's nuance.

Before trying to rewrite our stories, it's critical to normalize them. To understand that we're not broken. To make sense of

exactly who we are, in this moment. My first step toward healing was tracing back the lineage of what I'd learned about what
it meant to be a woman. To be attractive. The lessons I learned
about what sex is. What love is.

The overwhelming majority of my clients grew up learning
that sex—as a source of pleasure—is wrong. Some were raised
in sex-negative religions, espousing the virtue of waiting until
marriage.

My client Nina's grandmother had been forced to marry at
fourteen when she became pregnant. Her mom had her first kid
at sixteen. Neither of them finished high school.

But Nina wanted a different path. When we started working
together, she was in her thirties and finishing a PhD to become a
therapist. She and her husband had decided not to have kids, and
he'd recently undergone a vasectomy to make sure their plans
wouldn't get derailed.

She was hell-bent on not repeating the generational pattern
of becoming a martyr to motherhood.

But there were other deeply ingrained messages that still
haunted her and were holding her back from sexual pleasure. In
a nutshell, Nina didn't know how to speak up for herself or her
desires. "My husband asks me to initiate more, to tell him what
I want. But I have no idea how to put words to it. I feel awkward
and immature when I ask for sex, like I'm doing it wrong."

Once we dove deeper, it was clear that Nina had never been
allowed to ask for what she wanted, in or out of the bedroom.
She grew up in a chaotic household and was told she was too
much, emotionally. "I was pressured to keep quiet, to not be
myself." In hindsight, she now recognizes she was a child living

with undiagnosed ADHD as a child. And instead of seeking out treatment, her parents "shamed and ignored" her. "I had to be seen and not heard."

So she was forced to develop her own coping mechanisms: by becoming hyper independent and not expecting—or asking for—help. This forced silence followed her into her marriage. Not only did she struggle to express her sexual needs, she felt like a burden requesting most types of emotional support and intimacy. Even expressing positive emotions was difficult in her marriage.

"We tell each other we love each other...and then the conversation just stops. It never goes any deeper than that."

We took a look at her 27 Things list, and I noticed something: "I want to speak to him in Spanish while we make love."

I asked her to elaborate. She explained they'd been in the same college Spanish class early in their relationship and used to practice speaking it together. Back then, things were simpler, more romantic. But she was admittedly rusty now when it came to speaking the language.

I asked if she had any ideas for how to bring their Spanish connection and deeper intimacy back into the relationship. "He actually bought me a book of poetry written in Spanish, but with English translations."

Perfect.

At my urging, she texted him during our session, asking him if they could look through the book together later that night and pick a poem to read for the other.

And then...crickets.

During our next session a week later, Nina felt deflated. She'd put herself out there—with an ask that was very much outside her comfort zone—and her husband hadn't taken the bait. And not surprisingly, she didn't bring it up to him again. His silence was confirmation of the messaging she'd had since she was a kid: don't ask people for support.

But I'm pretty relentless as a coach and wasn't about to let her throw the intimacy baby out with the bathwater.

Instead, we found the babiest step we could to get their conversations moving toward the deep end of the pool. They had a routine of texting each other "I love you" throughout the day. I encouraged Nina to shoot him a text with an "I love you *because...*"

"I love you because you're so loving to me and Luna [their dog]." She hit Send.

And then we waited.

She was scared. And as someone who'd been in schooling for years to become a therapist, she knew exactly why. "My parents never modeled for me how to express love, so of course I don't know how to do it."

"You don't know how to do it *yet*," I reminded her.

And then her phone buzzed.

"I love you because you're so in touch with your emotions," read her husband's response.

And when I tell you Nina burst into tears, I'm not exaggerating. This wasn't just evidence that she could ask for connection and get a response; this was real-world proof that her emotions weren't too much. In fact, they were exactly *why* her husband loved her.

"This is one of those core moments of rewriting that scary thing into something doable and rewarding," she messaged me later that day. And I couldn't have said it better myself.

Because baby steps—"moments," as Nina put them—are what make up our lives. This wasn't the end of her journey of deeper intimacy and connection; it was the beginning of it.

But here's the catch: if you don't take the time to get *really* clear on what your current story is, there's no way you can effectively rewrite it. A mentor of mine likes to say, "Don't hand out Band-Aids for a bleeding neck problem." Your underlying story is the bleeding neck problem. So instead of handing you a Band-Aid—"Just use this app and you'll be fine!"—we're going to go in and assess the wound. We're going to clean it and stitch it up. (And fear not! I'll be giving you an entire school nurse's supply of Band-Aids later in the book.)

Up next is the least fun assignment in this whole book. It'll take you some time to get through, and you might be *really* tempted to skip it. But you'll be doing yourself a disservice if you do—I promise.

External Messaging Inventory

Who we are as intimate beings is a product of the messaging we grew up with. Whether that be messaging from our family, our culture, or our religious upbringing, we have absorbed many of those messages. By choosing to live our lives differently from what's dictated by our messaging, we become susceptible to feelings of shame.

One way to begin dissolving these feelings of shame is to boil these messages down to clear, concise statements. Once we have those statements, we can turn to who those statements came from. We then ask, has this person done the thing I am trying to do? Finally, we attempt to see their messaging as coming from a different lens than ours.

Coming to realize we are all doing the best we can with the tools we currently have provides us compassion for others and grace for our own journeys. Our toolboxes are different from theirs and are ever growing.

Here's your inventory to complete, including some examples from prior Shameless clients.

A WOMAN'S ROLE

What external message did you receive about what a woman's role is?

Hold everything together. Be responsible. Don't be needy. Take care of others. Don't take up too much space or demand anything for yourself.

Who did that message come from?

My mom.

Has this person done the thing you are trying to do?

No. She (at least mostly) gave up on intimacy in her life.

In what way is this person's lens different from yours, such that you can see where their messaging comes from?

She had a father who made her feel like she wasn't good enough. She grew up in a different time. Her mom died when my sister and I were little. My mom didn't have much support (emotional or actual/practical). She probably felt pretty alone.

SEX

What external message did you receive about sex?

That it is wrong, dirty, unspeakable...outside marriage. And anything "adventurous" is shameful and how dare you even have those thoughts.

Who did that message come from?

My mother.

Has this person done the thing you are trying to do?

She has not. She has a horrible, loveless marriage because she refuses to acknowledge there are problems...much less get help.

In what way is this person's lens different from yours, such that you can see where their messaging comes from?

Again, it goes back to her inability to carry out healthy relationships. I know in my head that nothing my mother tells me I should ever listen to.

FEELINGS/EMOTIONS

What external message did you receive about expressing feelings and emotions?

Stupid child (meaning nobody cares about your feelings).

Who did that message come from?

My mother.

Has this person done the thing you are trying to do?

I doubt my mother has done any introspective therapy or looked at how she acted/reacted to her children.

In what way is this person's lens different from yours, such that you can see where their messaging comes from?

My mother grew up in an upper-middle-class family. She had polio as a child. She was spoiled and taken care of as she grew up. I have heard stories from my aunt of how my grandmother was mean and would pinch her and would make her shake her bra after babysitting to make sure my aunt gave her all the babysitting money. I thought my mother was the "good" daughter who they spoiled. But I really do not know. I know my grandmother and mother did not talk for years. As a child, I would have to be on the phone with my grandmother and tell my mom what Grandma said and vice versa.

PHYSICAL BEAUTY

What external messages did you receive about what constitutes a physically attractive woman?

Small, flawless, quiet, dainty, effortless, luscious hair, clear smooth skin.

Who did that message come from?

Mostly my mother commenting on beautiful women on shows and movies. My dad would comment on what is seen as attractive for women. Just the other day, he was talking about women getting muscular and how they can take it too far and it becomes unattractive. Or that big tattoos are unattractive on women. I have two huge tattoos lol.

Has this person done the thing you are trying to do?

No, my mother is still very self-conscious and hates her husband. My dad is extremely fear based and perpetually single.

In what way is this person's lens different from yours, such that you can see where their messaging comes from?

My mother didn't have anyone to look up to for healthy self-image and so she could only go off what she saw in media. My dad sees through a conservative lens that hopes and dreams of perfection and never looks at flaws as beauty.

LOVE AND RELATIONSHIPS

What external messages did you receive about love and relationships?

My parents discouraged me from dating and pursuing relationships until I left their home. They would have preferred for me to be in an arranged marriage or married someone who was Tamil.

Who did that message come from?

My parents.

Has this person done the thing you are trying to do?

No, they were married by astrology/family dictates. They had no agency.

In what way is this person's lens different from yours, such that you can see where their messaging comes from?

I've had agency to dictate the course of my life.

Your Life Story

Now that the puzzle pieces are laid out, it's time to reconfigure them. Write a brief story of your life, incorporating the external messaging you received. Make yourself the hero of this story, highlighting the courageous and brave woman you are today. I encourage you to aim for five hundred words, but trust your gut!

If you're having a standoff with a blank page (or screen), try starting at the end and working your way backward chronologically. Where are you right *now*? How have you changed, or how are you *wanting* to change? How are you committed to breaking free from your mold?

3

Give Your Trauma a Home

When I was four years old, my female nanny put a crayon into my vagina.

When I was sixteen years old, I woke up to a male friend having sex with me.

Between the ages of twenty-five and thirty-eight, I interviewed hundreds of women and children who recounted—in graphic detail—the horrific sexual abuses they'd suffered.

You'd think that's where my trauma came from. Having lived it. Having witnessed it. Having absorbed it.

The reality is there's no such thing as a universally traumatic event. It's how our bodies *respond* to an event that classifies it as trauma. An ER doctor may see people die on a daily basis and not respond but hyperventilate at the sight of a loved one perishing. Hearing gunshots, a cop will react differently to the sound than a survivor of a school shooting.

In other words, don't assume that because a person has

witnessed or experienced something horrific, their brain has interpreted the event (or events) as traumas. And—on the flip side—never underestimate the power of a seemingly innocuous occurrence to send someone into a full-blown trauma response.

I was reminded of this as I sat in the back of an Uber, sobbing and shaking uncontrollably. I'd just left a professional event for the Westside Bar Association (WBA), an event attended by a few hundred lawyers who were interested in networking and meeting their continuing education requirements. An event that—for all intents and purposes—should have been pretty boring.

And that was why I'd agreed to speak on the panel. The focus of the night was *The Staircase*, a 2004 docuseries that had garnered newfound interest due to a recent Netflix re-release. WBA had successfully leveraged the popularity of other Netflix series for similar events in the past: they'd brought in Amanda Knox the prior year and the attorneys for Steven Avery (of *Making a Murderer* notoriety) the year before.

When the head of the WBA had initially asked me to speak on the panel, I said no. "Why would I put myself on a stage and talk about a case I have zero connection to?" He told me David Rudolf (the original defense attorney) would be there too, along with a few coroners and a blood spatter expert. "You're such a likable and personable force in the DA's Office. It would be great to have a prosecutor on the stage to give the audience some other information to chew on. Plus, David will *love* you," he assured me.

"I'll do it on one condition. I want to sit next to a live owl on stage." There was an alternate theory in the murder case involving an owl, so the request was apropos but also totally inconceivable. Until it wasn't.

"We've secured the owl. Can't wait to have you!"

Fuck.

So I started preparing. I rewatched the entire docuseries. I listened to hours upon hours of a BBC podcast that discussed evidence that hadn't been presented on screen. I wove all this information into a well-crafted speech about the dangers of labeling entertainment as "true" crime and the filmmakers' strategic decision to include very little information about the woman who'd been murdered. I pointed out that we live in Los Angeles, that the event itself was held in Hollywood—a place of stories—and that what we'd been binge-watching had been nothing more than that: a story.

And I did a fantastic job.

The audience cheered.

And then David Rudolf lost his shit on me.

He stood up and called me unethical. He questioned the very reputation I'd worked over a decade to build at the DA's Office—the same reputation that had gotten me invited onto this stage in the first place. What was meant to be a professional event turned into—as one attorney said on Facebook the next day—"an MMA match."

Don't get me wrong: I was used to going toe-to-toe with vigorous defense attorneys in court. I was no stranger to opposing viewpoints. I'd chosen a career based on an adversarial search for the truth.

But I wasn't used to having a man stand up aggressively and yell at me in a place where I was supposed to feel safe.

Or was I?

When I was twenty, I married a man I'd fallen in love with

while I was studying abroad in the UK. Our five-year marriage devolved into a nightmare of raised voices and resentment. I was in a constant state of vigilance, waiting for the other shoe to drop, for him to explode on me. And over the course of those years, my body protected me by completely shutting down. I'd go silent, which had the perverse effect of making him even more angry.

And as I sat next to that owl on stage, my brain reverted back to what it had done over a decade before. I fell silent. I let him yell and scream. I did not engage.

Many of us think of fight or flight as trauma responses, but freeze is one of the most difficult to understand. We essentially "play dead" so that our predators will leave us alone.

And that's what I'd done...in front of a few hundred people. After the event ended, I was surrounded by friends, family, and colleagues who kept repeating how much ass I'd kicked. To this day, whenever people bring up that night fondly, I have to correct them: "That's one of the most traumatic events I've ever experienced." And they don't understand.

Even typing this right now is bringing up uncomfortable sensations in my body. I want to stop what I'm doing and cry uncontrollably.

A few weeks after the event, I went to the movies alone and a fight almost broke out. A well-known figure in the LA community who had recently been outed as an abuser (this was the #MeToo era) had been spotted in the back of the theater, and a mob of angry men formed about fifteen feet from where I sat with my popcorn. The parties involved were escorted out. The danger was removed, but I shook through the entire movie. Then I came home and cried.

I called a friend who works in film. I sobbed and recounted what had transpired. And he didn't understand.

When I'm interviewed on podcasts and mention I'm a childhood and teenage sexual assault survivor, they think they understand. Sexual abuse is one of those catchalls that just screams trauma. But I can count on one hand the number of times I've been triggered during sex, and I've lost count of how many times I've been triggered by no-big-deal situations.

Again, the act itself doesn't define the trauma. It's how our body *reacts* to it.*

In her book *Unbroken: The Trauma Response Is Never Wrong*, Dr. MaryCatherine McDonald defines trauma as an experience or set of experiences that both causes unbearable emotions and lacks a relational home.

To illustrate, I like to think of trauma as a pile of clothes sitting on the bed that needs to be folded and put away. Avoiding the pile (or the trauma) won't make it disappear. Instead, you need some Marie Kondo tips for your trauma to start folding and organizing your emotional pile.

I've seen trauma manifest in a variety of ways with clients. Because of my background as a sex crimes and domestic violence prosecutor, a not insignificant number of women who come to me are assault or abuse survivors. And their type of abuse varies. I've worked with women who suffered years of spousal rape.

---

* I definitely can't give the vast universe of trauma its deserving bandwidth in one single lesson. If you want a heavy (both in terms of length and breadth!) read on the subject, I'll point you to Bessel van der Kolk's *The Body Keeps the Score*, which is basically the trauma bible. If you're looking for an equally comprehensive but more approachable book (complete with personal and client stories, like this one!), *Unbroken* by MaryCatherine McDonald is for you. If you want to dive deeper into pleasure after sexual trauma specifically, Dr. Holly Richmond's *Reclaiming Pleasure* is your next stop.

Clients who were molested by their biological fathers. Girlfriends who were called worthless pieces of shit by their partners for years on end.

But their trauma responses were unique to them. Some—like me—would shut down when they were criticized or yelled at. One client would begin crying during sex in missionary position. Several would shake whenever they were touched on certain parts of their body.

One client of mine, Iselda, had been abused by her tennis coach as a teenager for years. He always paid special attention to her legs, a part of her body that gave him easy access thanks to the short tennis skirts she'd wear. He would stroke them, tell her how beautiful they were. And that was his systematic way of initiating further abuse on the rest of her body.

Another client, Brenda, was repeatedly molested by her cousin when she was a young child. He would force her to perform oral sex on him and would then ejaculate on her stomach.

I guide all my clients through a process of "G-rated" (i.e., non-sexual) self-touch during our work together (you'll be practicing this yourself later in the book). We turn our computer cameras off, and I direct them to use their hands to get curious about their bodies: What type of sensation, pressure, and touch feels good? What doesn't? They then talk me through their findings.

Both Iselda and Brenda were triggered during the exercise: Iselda when she touched her legs and Brenda when she touched her stomach. Both were brought right back to the abuse they'd suffered decades before. Neither had expected this reaction.

There's the misconception that our triggers are something to be avoided. That would look something like, "Hey, I don't like it when you touch my stomach. Can you not do that?" And yes, that will avoid the trauma response, but it doesn't work through it. Pushing your laundry pile to one side of the bed so you can sleep at night isn't the same as folding it and putting it away in its "home."

McDonald reminds us there aren't any hard and fast rules to defining what a relational home actually is. My goal in working with trauma survivors is to essentially house hunt. We do this by sending *new* data to their brains, data that says, "That was then. This is now. This part of my body is not only safe to touch, it can be a source of pleasure." And we do this incrementally.

In the cases of Iselda and Brenda, I tasked them with spending some time on their own, focusing solely on the body part in question. "Keep your eyes open, and gently caress that part of your body. Repeat—either out loud or in your mind—'I am safe.' Be gentle with yourself. If you start getting triggered, stop. Then try again tomorrow."

By the time we finished our work together, both women had reestablished a loving relationship with all parts of their bodies. They saw their bodies as part of them, as the home they inhabit. But it didn't happen overnight, and it's important to understand that this is a process. Note that I didn't suggest that either of them ask a partner to touch them. This was self-guided. It was challenging at first, of course. They were rewiring decades' worth of armor their brains and bodies had piled on to make them feel safe.

Baby steps are key here. Say, for example, you'd gotten into a terrible car accident while driving on the freeway. You'd very understandably be scared as hell the next time you got behind the wheel. So do you just avoid driving for the rest of your life? I mean, that's one solution. If—like me—you live in a city where that's unrealistic ("Nobody Walks in LA," after all), you'd rewrite that narrative in increments. You'd start off by getting into the car and sitting behind the wheel.

"Oh, I didn't get hurt. This is safe," your brain would calculate.

Then you'd take a spin around the block. Then you'd drive a few miles on city streets. Then you'd get on the freeway for the span of one exit. And so forth. You'd incrementally give your brain new data that says, "I'm not going to get into a car wreck every time I get behind the wheel."

The same is true for any other trigger. We want to restage the trauma, in the same way a theater producer might alter a story on an actual stage. We're putting the same play on, but maybe it's set on a summer's day in a park instead of a battle-field. Perhaps the victim becomes the heroine. Maybe there's a plot twist at the end.

It's the same story, but we're telling it a little differently. And here's the rub: we can't think our way through this. Your thoughts didn't cause the trauma, and they won't restage the trauma. Trauma is an *event* (or series of events), and as such, you need *new events* for your brain to know you're safe.

Start by recognizing your triggers. In Iselda's and Brenda's cases, it was having a particular part of their bodies touched. In my case, it was being in a place I assumed was safe (a professional event, a movie theater) where men lost control and raised their voices.

Once you've recognized your triggers, ask yourself: What's the story here? And write it down. For them, it was "I'm being abused if this part of my body is touched." For me, it was "Men who raise their voices will hurt me."

Now, think of a way you can *restage* that story. The work I did with Iselda and Brenda led them to a new narrative: "I am in control of my body, and it can receive pleasure."

Because there are myriad sources of trauma and triggers, I'll illustrate this concept by way of additional Shameless clients, all of whom have managed to lean into their triggers and give their traumas a home.

————

Irene was molested repeatedly by her father at a young age, most of which consisted of him performing oral sex on her. Now happily married, she wouldn't let her husband do the same. We used fantasy and role-play (which you'll learn about in a later lesson) to restage the trauma. She assumed a dominant role in the bedroom as a part of play and directed her husband to give her oral sex for a few weeks in a row.

- The original story: "Oral sex is something done to me against my will by someone who is abusing me."
- The restaged story: "Oral sex is something I can choose to experience that brings me pleasure."

Shayna was in a relationship for a decade with a man with whom she had two children. After she became a mother, he criticized the way her body had changed and told her she needed to get a tummy tuck and a breast lift to be attractive again. All the while, he would push her on the bed and force her to have sex against her will. Now in a healthy relationship, she was shutting down—shaking, crying—every time her new boyfriend initiated sex. We dissected what the specific triggers were: her boyfriend removing her clothes and him being on top of her in missionary position. She asked him if, for the time being, she could be the one to take off her own clothes and if they could take missionary off the table and explore some other positions. In a matter of weeks, she started leaning into requesting that he take off her clothes and requesting missionary position.

- The original story: "When someone else takes off my clothes and has sex on top of me, it's against my will."
- The restaged story: "I have control over my body and my clothing, and having sex—in any position—is my choice."

Ana had been emotionally neglected by the men in her life, first with a father who would leave her in the car while he drank inside bars, then with a brother whose schizophrenic outbursts left her in a constant state of fear. As a result, she was distrustful of having romantic relationships with men. To rewrite her story, she made a list of five men every day who she considered to be "safe." These ranged from coworkers to friends to Barack Obama (for real). She eventually started scheduling phone calls with some of these men (not Obama, obviously) to reinforce that she was, in fact, surrounded by evidence to refute her original story.

- The original story: "Men are unsafe."
- The restaged story: "Some men are unsafe, but most of them aren't."

Leigh was raped on a beach when she was sixteen. Despite living within driving distance of the coast her whole life (she's now in her fifties), she'd never gone back to swim in the ocean. But she was drawn to the water and loved watching YouTube surfing videos and underwater nature documentaries for fun. During our time together, she signed up for surf lessons and now attends them regularly.

- The original story: "The beach is dangerous, and my body doesn't belong to me when I'm there."
- The restaged story: "The ocean is a place of beauty, and my body is a vessel to experience it."

Now that you have a general feel for how to restage the story (or stories!) you've written down, jot down a few ideas for baby steps you can take to start you on your journey. Commit to getting one action item on the calendar this week.

You may be wondering how you can effectively restage your story without re*living* it. And here's the deal: remove the X factor that made it dangerous in the first place. Touch yourself instead of having another person touch you. Create the scenario where *you* are in the director's chair. You'll notice from the examples I gave, every single one of these clients had complete agency throughout their restaging: Leigh scheduled her own surf lesson and could've called it quits. Shayna requested oral sex instead of it being forced on her. Patience and baby steps are key here.

I'll bring it back to me for a moment, because you might be wondering how I restaged the event I mentioned to you earlier (and no, it wasn't by hanging out with more owls).

You're reading it.

As I finished recounting my personal story earlier in this lesson, I texted my partner a photo of what I'd written, accompanied with "Wrote a thousand words of this and now I need a break. No bueno." I gave myself permission to take a break... but then I kept going. The *Staircase* panel had been a triggering event for me for years; any mention of it would make my pulse rise and give me flashbacks of cowering on a stage while a man berated me.

But there's a new story now, isn't there?

"Yes, men may yell at me. They can dent me, but they can't break me. And I can shine a light on those dents as a way to help others."

I can't wave a magic wand and eliminate loud men from the face of the earth. But moving forward, my brain knows there's a drawer I can put their screams into.

In discussing my story here with you, I've given it a home. Thank you.

Rip Off Your Armor

n my final year of law school, I was accepted into a trial advocacy class designed for folks (like me) who had dreams of becoming prosecutors. For one of our final assignments, we were placed inside a mock courtroom with cameras and tasked with cross-examining a witness. On a later date, each of us would meet individually with our professor and watch the video together, eagerly awaiting her feedback on our performance.

"You may want to consider not wearing black suits in court" was how she started the meeting. "You have a really strong presence, and the last thing you want is for a jury to dismiss you for being the stereotypical 'bitch DA.' Maybe opt for a brown or royal-blue suit instead."

I was horrified. Not just because she'd made her entire critique about me being "too much" but because I knew she was right. Watching the video, I did look like a bitch. The meat of my questioning—my performance—was an A, but my demeanor was a C-.

This was what I got for checking out library books on "how to win at cross-examination." For writing op-ed pieces during high school journalism that won awards. For being paid $20 per A on my report card in elementary school (and having the amount doubled if I got straight A's).

I'd been rewarded my entire life for being emotionless. For being a perfectionist. For working hard and performing. And it all came crumbling down the moment my professor told me that being emotionless isn't what'll reward you in a courtroom—the place I dreamed of spending my professional career.

And the struggle didn't end. Once my dream came true—once I became a trial attorney—I was forced to walk a delicate tightrope of being authoritative and trustworthy, human and infallible, feminine but not bitchy. I would sit across from children disclosing horrible sexual and physical abuse and hide my shock to maintain my professional distance. And when it came time for trial, I'd eventually have to show just the right amount of emotion to get a jury to care but not so much that they perceived me as a loose cannon. I wore tailored skirt suits that conveyed an air of being polished but unsexy. I never took my blazer off—even when the AC broke down during a summer heat wave—because I was worried my conservative colleagues would think less of me once they realized I have tattoos.

Full-time employees spend more time working than we do with the people we love. It only made sense that I was taking this hardened exterior with me into relationships. It isn't a switch we can turn off at a whim; it's the wire buried in the walls.

And my wires ran deep. I couldn't say "I love you" to my friends. I would cringe if things got too close, too intimate. I was able to let loose during random sex with strangers but would shut down in a long-term relationship. Nearly twenty years ago, a partner said to me, "I'm not actually convinced you'll ever be able to have kids. I'm not actually convinced you're a woman."

If I wanted to change, I needed to tear down the drywall and replace those electrical wires. If I wanted intimacy, I would need to learn how to become vulnerable. And yes, I could read all the Brené Brown (the world's leading researcher on shame and vulnerability) books in the world, but unless I knew how to begin practicing it, I was doomed to a life of surface-level relationships at best and not actually knowing who the fuck I was at worst. Self-help is just *shelf help* unless you're willing to put in the reps.

In my final year as a prosecutor, I was assigned to an elite unit in the DA's Office that prosecutes law enforcement. In that role, I was placed as co-counsel on a case that was one of the most high profile in our unit: the first officer-involved shooting the DA's Office had prosecuted in roughly two decades. My boss told me the assignment was a "reward" for the hard work I'd been doing. I had flashbacks of the riots that followed the Rodney King verdict: my elementary school being closed, looking down at the city from my childhood home, a blanket of smoke much thicker than the smog that is our daily here in LA. I didn't want to play a role in widespread anguish and civil unrest, and I sure as hell didn't want my face all over the papers (my "reward") over a case I was almost certain would result in a not guilty verdict for the officer.

And as the case inched its way to trial, the world was in a state of chaos. A pandemic had hit. Protests over the police killing George Floyd were waging all around the country. We had curfews citywide here in LA, and I could hear helicopters swarming over my apartment all hours of the night. People were camping out in front of elected officials' homes. I literally had nightmares about what would happen to me—a woman, living alone—if a jury didn't return a guilty verdict in this case. While most other folks were putting on weight during the pandemic, I lost nearly ten pounds in the span of a month.

Something had to give. I scheduled an in-office meeting with my bosses the next day. I spent the evening before rewatching Brené Brown's *The Call to Courage* documentary to mentally prepare for the uncharacteristic vulnerability I'd have to present. I promised myself I would go into the arena with courage. I'd be prepared for the blood, sweat, and tears.

And there were a lot of tears once the office door closed. A cathartic ending to a stress cycle that'd been going on for months. "I won't be able to show up for myself—much less this job—if I can't sleep at night," I managed to sputter out. "I don't have the strength for this."

They didn't try to talk me out of it. They immediately offered to reassign the case and then asked how they could best support me.[†]

It turns out I'd made assumptions about all DAs. Since I switched careers, many have reached out to me, not just to congratulate me on my newfound calling but to ask for sex toy recommendations, disclose their swinging tendencies, and even request help designing a sex room. They're not all heartless shells of humans. They're actually a lot more like me than I'd ever known. It turns out I'd told myself a lie about who I was supposed to be. And I'd been living that lie for most of my adult life.

---

† In case you're curious, the officer was, in fact, found not guilty. There was no ensuing civil unrest

As such, I have a special place in my heart for a certain type of client: high-performing women who've put up walls in their professional lives that remained in place in their personal lives. Women who never had any issue finding a partner but who retreated into their shells once the relationship got too intimate.

Women who remind me of me.

So when Marie came to me and explained her predicament, I felt an immediate affinity for her. "I feel stuck and scared of admitting to myself and showing others I need them. The more I like someone, the further away I will stay."

During our consultation, she recounted a story about a man she'd met recently on a dating app. They'd had hot, kinky sex at his place. After they were done, he asked her if she wanted to stick around to have some dinner and watch an episode of *The Simpsons*. And it made her skin crawl.

She'd never had an issue meeting men to have sex with. Being sexually open and feeling liberated wasn't what was holding her back: it was the postscript. The part where the afterglow settles and two people are left sitting there as their true, raw selves. That part scared the fuck out of her. She had no idea how to be vulnerable. How to let down her guard and show up as her true self—not just in dating and romantic relationships but in all her relationships.

Marie works in theater and travels with casts and productions regularly. She couldn't form relationships with the people who acted as her temporary family. She'd just as easily write them off as snobby than actually make an effort to connect with them. She isolated from them, retreating to her hotel room and using dating apps city to city to make temporary and fleeting connections through one-night stands. And as a result, she felt lonely much of her waking life.

When we started working together, she'd been in therapy for almost five years. She'd made progress in a lot of ways but still struggled to see the best in people...including herself.

Many women don't walk around using the word *shame* to describe how we feel about ourselves. Why? Because shame sounds so...yucky. Most of us would rather say, "I would feel *guilty* for speaking up for what I need. I would feel *scared* of being rejected." We use the terms *guilt* and *fear* as substitutes for the exact word that means "I'm not worthy. My needs aren't as valuable as others'. There's something wrong with me."

But Marie used the term *shame* often. She could see very clearly how shame held her back. When she was asked to complete a writing exercise about what her life would look like if shame *weren't* an option, the floodgates opened.

———

"If shame wasn't an option, I wouldn't stop myself from making connections with people for fear that they would not like me, would judge me, or that I would be annoying them in some way. If it wasn't for shame, I wouldn't even mind people disliking me because I would know it wasn't a fault of mine but just a fact of life and that like and dislike are only one way in which we connect with people and think about them. Without shame, I would see the world as an open opportunity where anything is possible and that wherever and however you end up living is the right way. If I didn't feel shame, I wouldn't see feedback as a threat. I wouldn't see it

as a mean way for someone to try and rise above me, again
to change my world for the worse, to show me up."

———————

Marie had developed thick armor to keep other people out for
fear of being hurt. And she was dying to rip that armor off and let
the mangled shards of metal drop to the floor. But allowing that
to happen was even more terrifying.

The armor that protects you from a knife in your back also
stops a caress on the cheek. Sunblock will shield you from the
sun's harmful rays, but we still need vitamin D to survive. Whether
you feel safe or not, being intimate requires vulnerability. And
fortunately, there are some ways to start identifying the type of
armor you're wearing and how to begin gently prying it off you.

Muting

You know the mute button on your remote control? The one you
click when those annoying commercials pop on? There's a good
chance you're doing things on a regular basis to hit the emotional
mute button, to tune out the pestering thoughts.

When you think of muting, you might conjure up images of
getting blackout drunk or eating an entire pizza by yourself. And
yes, those can be acts of muting. But so can working. Or exercis-
ing. Or needing to be social all the time. Or spending as much
time as you can helping other people. It's not the action itself that
makes it muting or not muting; it's the *why* behind the action.

I describe muting as anything we do to avoid sitting with the
hard feelings. I've personally muted myself in all of the above ways to

avoid having to think about everything ranging from my dissatisfaction with my marriage to the ambivalence I'd come to feel in my job.

Imagine this: you're in a completely empty room with no distractions whatsoever. Where does your mind go? Where does it spiral to? What's the darkest thought you have?

That's what you're trying to mute.

Marie summed up her muting as follows: "I had an eating disorder when I was younger. It got so bad my period stopped for two years. I was fasting and bingeing and would spend two to three hours a day at the gym. Even now, I really have to fight the urge to starve myself if I've eaten a lot the day before. It happens when I'm home alone. I start to feel lonely and wonder: am I unlovable?"

I am unlovable. That was what she was trying to mute. That was the thought she was scared of sitting alone with.

And here's the thing with our fears: Once we identify them, either they're not as bad as we thought they'd be, or they're pretty unlikely to happen.

With Marie, being unlovable unearthed the root fear that—as an unlovable person—she would end up dying alone. This is one of the most common root fears I see with the clients I've worked with and definitely falls into the second category above.

So I asked her the same question I've asked other clients with that fear: "On a scale of one to ten, what's the likelihood of you actually dying alone?"

And her response was also typical of what I've seen: "I have wonderful friends and family. Even if I didn't end up having a partner, I wouldn't really be alone, would I? I'd rank it about a one."

When we can reframe our fears in those terms, we can make sense of where we assign our mental bandwidth. When the chances of our fears actually materializing are on par with being struck by lightning, we can have control over our fears instead of them controlling us. I'll be showing you a daily practice on how to make peace with your fears later in this lesson.

Brickwalling

My partner and I were at a Charlotte Gainsbourg concert early on in our relationship. He stood behind me, his arms enveloping my waist, our bodies moving in slow unison. My ex-husband wasn't super into concerts. And what I felt having this wonderful man hold me as I watched one of my favorite musicians was pure, overwhelming...*joy.*

And I couldn't fucking deal with it.

I swiveled my head around and whispered in his ear, "Can you just promise me that if you break up with me, you'll at least give me some advanced warning?"

"Come with me," he said, linking his arm through mine. He escorted me into the quieter lobby of the concert venue.

And then he called me on my shit.

"You're building a wall right now, brick by brick," he told me, "and you're driving a care right into it."

I wish I'd had a photo of the expression on my face, the absolute shock and horror of being so completely understood.

And that, my friends, is what I call brickwalling. It's not being able to deal with happiness. It's being so scared of losing something that your mind immediately fast-forwards to the tragic ending, hoping to reverse engineer the present in order to avoid the future.

Brickwalling isn't as common as the other types of vulnerability armor. Some clients have looked at me quizzically when I've explained the concept to them ("I love joy!" they say). And others bow their heads solemnly with the satisfaction of knowing their experience is common enough that there's actually a term for it.

Marie fell into the latter category. "I undercut joy and try to find the problem in it. I actually had a job opportunity come up recently, and instead of telling my friends how excited I was I made it out like it was no big deal."

When it comes to dating and intimacy, brickwalling can also look like "I don't want to get excited about her because she'll probably just end up ghosting me." And while this line of thinking may seem kind of logical on its surface, there's something devastating below it: *you lose the joy entirely*.

When you catch your mind doing that sneaky thing, notice it. And noticing it can look like, "Fuck, I'm doing that thing where I'm trying to beat tragedy to the punch!" And then ask yourself, "What emotions am I missing out on in this moment by turning to fear?"

For me, it was more joy of being with a man I love listening to music I love. For Marie, it was the buzzing excitement that comes along with sharing life events with people who are important to her.

And those are the good, delicious parts of life. Those are *why* we are alive.

Perfectionism

Oh, lordy lord. I could perhaps write a whole book on this one. (And if you'd like to *read* an entire book about it, pick up a copy of Brené Brown's *The Gifts of Imperfection*.) Perfectionism is the single most common trait I see among my clients.

Read. That. Again.

When I ask, "How does perfectionism show up in your life?" I'm often met with "How much time do you have?" or "How does perfectionism *not* show up in my life?"

And let's be real: up until fairly recently, saying "I'm a bit of a perfectionist!" was some sort of badge of honor. Not having a hair out of place. Throwing a Pinterest-perfect party. You know what I'm talking about.

The trend I'm now seeing is the idea of being "perfectly imperfect." Which is a step in the right direction but still misses the mark. I'm here to give a huge middle finger to this idea of perfect, as I believe it's one of the most insidious afflictions we as humans suffer from today.

Perfection is absolute garbage. And if you remember one thing from this book, remember this:

You cannot experience intimacy as a perfectionist.

Why? Because being a perfectionist is saying "I'm not enough as I am. I have to perform and act and wear a mask and be someone else in order to be accepted." And guess what? You'll never be able to connect intimately with another human being if you're walking around wearing a mask. This isn't Halloween, people. This is your life.

How many experiences in your life have you missed out on because of perfectionism? Maybe it was picking up a store-bought cake because you didn't trust how a homemade one would turn out. Maybe it was not wearing a bikini to the beach because you have stomach rolls. Maybe it was drafting an email a dozen times and never hitting send...and missing out on a potential positive outcome waiting for you on the other end.

Marie had tricked herself into thinking of perfectionism as "just good work ethic." And as a result, she couldn't handle criticism from her colleagues. As you now know, she couldn't forge human connections with them either. We needed to make a plan.

Gratitude is an antidote to perfectionism. It's a way of saying "I'm not an island. I'm not doing this alone. Thank you for being here." In a world where we're expected to do it all, to know it all (and to look great while doing and knowing it all), expressing gratitude to other people is an act of rebellion. Every time you do it, you're sending new data to your brain that says, "Hey, it's okay to need people!" while also showing those around you that you're not a Pinterest-perfect cardboard cutout of a human being.

So as one of her homework assignments, Marie sent out a daily gratitude text for a week to either a coworker or a friend. This was a huge stretch for her, but it became easier over time. And it wasn't just the texting that became easier; her view of the world began to shift. "I actually started to spot moments in real time where I could say thanks to them. *I rewired more in a week than I did in all my time in therapy.*" Once her emotions had been recalibrated toward gratitude, she constantly saw opportunities to express it. Like exercise, gratitude is a practice and not just a one and done. But committing to it (I'll show you how below!) will turn it into second nature.

All right, so maybe you don't identify as a perfectionist. "I *know* I'm not perfect, so why would I even *try* to be?" you may be thinking to yourself. But let me ask you: Are you someone who struggles to ask for help?

Poker players have tells when they're bluffing. When it comes to perfectionism, resisting asking for help is a huge tell.

Sometimes folks don't ask for help because they think they can do it better themselves. But very often, people won't ask for help *because they want to be perceived as having their shit together*. And when we signal to folks that we don't, it reveals a crack in our veneer and—holy crap!—a real, living human being underneath.

But let me flip it on you. It feels good to help people, right? And I'm not talking about feeding the homeless every Thanksgiving (we can't all be that person). I'm talking about being the person who gives your friend a book recommendation or a ride to the mechanic. I'm talking about being the person who offers a shoulder for a friend to smear mascara all over. Chances are you are a person who enjoys the joy that comes along with helping people. And here's the deal: *You are depriving other people of that same joy by doing everything yourself.*

Here's my challenge to perfectionists for a week:

Ask five people for help. It can be small (a book or restaurant recommendation) or big (help moving, a ride to the airport). Make a note of the following:

- Who you asked
- What you asked for
- What the response/outcome was

When you review these, you'll start to notice the support you do have and recast the story that asking for help is a sure-fire relationship ruiner.

And no matter what armor you're wearing, my other challenge to you is a three-part daily morning journal practice. I'm not here to tell you to journal every day for the rest of your life. I'm sharing with you my own journaling mindset practice that's changed *my* life and the lives of many women I've worked with. It's a quick combo to clear the fears out and recalibrate your gratitude meter. So try it for a week. If you hate it, it was only a week of your life. If you like some of it but not all of it? Take what you want, and leave the rest. Despite how many words you're about to read *explaining* the practice, once you sit down, it'll only take you about ten minutes.

Here's how you do it, in this order.

Fear Writing

Set a timer, and spend five minutes writing out all your fears or worries as a way to get the negative thoughts onto paper and out of your head. These can be larger/existential fears ("I will lose a family member") or smaller/more immediate worries ("my package won't arrive on time"). Do this stream-of-consciousness style.

"But, Rena, why am I going to ruminate over all the bad shit?"

Because fear is what encourages muting and discourages vulnerability and intimacy. Fear and worry are going to be there *regardless*, so let them live on the page instead of in your brain. Think of this as an emotional colonic (gross, I know). Let the shit out.

And like we saw with Marie, you'll probably find that when you let your worries out through a tantrum on the page, you'll realize the thing you're deeply afraid of isn't actually that bad, or it's bad, but it's really unlikely to happen.

What you'll also find is you keep repeating a lot of the same fears every day. *And you'll become bored with them.* I will literally

mutter to myself, "Oh, you're on *this* bullshit again?" when I
repeat the same fears for a few days in a row.

Once your emotional colonic is complete, it's time to move
on to the good stuff.

Gratitude

Write down three things you're grateful for in the following
format: "I'm grateful for X because Y."

There's an overwhelming amount of research in the field of
positive psychology about the correlation between experiencing
happiness and having a gratitude practice. I used to just write
down three things I was grateful for, and it often looked really
boring and generic. Like, how many times can I write that I'm
grateful for my partner? My career? My health? My family?

Adding the "because" is a game changer, because it gives you
space to express gratitude for the same things but in different ways:

- I'm grateful for my partner because he packed up leftovers
  for me to bring home.
- I'm grateful for my partner because he makes me feel seen.

- I'm grateful I'm my own boss because I can create a schedule
  that nourishes me.
- I'm grateful I'm my own boss because I can wear whatever
  I want to work.

But look for the small things to be grateful for too ("I'm grateful for Trader Joe's because I can buy really tasty premade meals"

is one that rings true to me). Bonus points if you can take something that appeared shitty on its surface and twist it, like this:

- I'm grateful I caught the flu because it's given me a chance to catch up on rest.

Now that you've expressed gratitude for the outside world, it's time to direct some of that love and attention toward yourself!

Brags

Write down five brags in the following format: "I am proud of myself for X because Y."

You think the fears make people uncomfortable? Many of my clients have a harder time bragging about themselves than wallowing in worry. Most women don't want to be perceived as arrogant or bitchy, so we downplay our accomplishments to make other people feel comfortable.

Fuck that.

If you're reading this book, it's because you don't want to keep living small, right?

Your journal is a sacred space, for your eyes only. My clients don't even share their journal entries with me. But I know it's easier to understand through example, so below are five actual brags from my own personal journal:

- I'm proud of myself for pushing out of my comfort zone with a new exercise regimen because I'm not scared of being a beginner.

- I'm proud of myself for taking Ativan when I need it because I don't have to be a martyr to my anxiety.
- I'm proud of myself for only eating three tacos last night because I stopped when I was satisfied and didn't eat out of boredom.
- I'm proud of myself for improving at flirting and making the first move with women because I'm not taking the stories I've told myself as truths.
- I'm proud of myself for taking a rest without shame because I trust I'll get my tasks done.

If you look closely, you'll see that brickwalling, perfectionism, and muting are undercurrents here. *I'm proud of myself when I don't do them.* With time, you will be too!

5

Harness Your 80-Year-Old Badass

'd left my husband. Between bouncing back and forth at a few friends' houses and staying at an Airbnb with an entire box worth of used condoms (left by the guest before me) in the trash can near the bed, I knew I needed a place to land.

But I was tired and hanging on by a thread. I needed something simple that wouldn't require me moving a bunch of things in or buying new furniture. And the universe provided: a furnished room in a Craftsman home in Franklin Hills, close to my favorite bars and restaurants. A roommate younger than me who had vintage vinyl Dolly Parton records and had painted the walls of the home pink. ("After my ex and I split up, I girlified the fuck out of the place!"). A magical backyard with an adjoining wall next to a washed-up Hollywood director who would get into loud screaming matches with his wife and their pet ducks (one of whom was named El Chapo) on a weekly basis.

It was perfect. A far cry from the home I'd shared with my

ex-husband in South Pasadena, a charming suburb of LA that we dubbed "the movie set" because it had so much picturesque, small-town charm (and movies are literally shot there all the time).

I'd been single before and gone balls to the wall. Late nights of partying and one-night stands. Packing into cars with bands from overseas and taking trips to Joshua Tree. I wanted it to be different this time. I wanted to find myself. I'd dropped a massive bomb in my life with the divorce, and instead of making snow angels in the ashes, I wanted to build my dream home.

So I started devouring as many self-help books as I could. I journaled a lot. I went to restorative yoga regularly at the studio around the corner. I had multiple sessions with a (not inexpensive) somatic body healer. And while I felt like I was doing all the damned things...I didn't feel like any of them were resonating. The phrase "your inner knowing" kept getting thrown around, but I couldn't fucking hear her.

In an effort to do *more* of all the things, I signed up to go to a full-moon sound bath up the street from my house. I didn't really understand what sound baths were, but I knew they were a thing people did when they were on their path to inner knowing and enlightenment, so I figured it was worth a shot. I turned down Friday-night offers of dinner, drinks, and what I would usually call "fun" to instead lie side by side with a bunch of strangers in a recreation room in a dilapidated building.

As I soon learned, the crystal bowls used in sound baths emit a sound that is supposed to get your body into a state that is in between being awake and being asleep. A space where your imagination is calling the shots. A space I now understand is where the subconscious—the part of the brain that controls most of our emotional operating systems—lives.

"Don't worry if you fall asleep," the soft-spoken leader said. "The waves will still heal your body however they need to."

That sounded like bullshit to me, but I'd already paid my thirty bucks.

And then we began. I can't describe to you how loud the sound from those crystal bowls is. So loud you can't hear yourself think. And there's a visceral pressure to the sound. I felt like it was pushing my body into the floor. Like in a dream where you have no control over your arms or legs. I felt paralyzed.

And then I chose to surrender. And what happened after is the closest thing I've experienced to being on drugs while not being on drugs.

I was a little girl, slaying a dragon. There were flames everywhere. I wore a yellow dress. And then a woman's voice—one I didn't recognize—said, "You have so much light to give."

"You have so much light to give."

"You have so much light to give."

Over and over again.

Tears came cascading down my face. Ugly ones. I could feel my mouth contorting, myself sobbing. I didn't know what the fuck was happening, but *something* was happening.

I cried until the tears ran out. Until I woke up from this half-asleep, half-awake state. And I knew I'd done the work I needed to do.

I absolutely hate the part in certain self-help books when the author has their "bodhi tree" moment. "I went and sat quietly somewhere and then—boom!—I had some batshit-crazy experience, and now I'm enlightened and I'll live happily ever after!" And you might think that's what I just described to you. But I want to set the record straight: while that was *a* pivotal moment, it wasn't *the* pivotal moment. Because there's no such thing. I'd be a charlatan if I told you that one single experience is all you'd need to transform yourself *forever*.

But in that hour, I felt like I'd made huge strides with the little version of me. The one who'd been rewarded for acting older than her age. She'd fought dragons her entire life and was now being told "Just be." She was told she is enough, that she has so much light to give.

I'd always had to put up a hard exterior. As a child, I was moved from kindergarten to fourth grade during reading hour. My TV watching was a combination of *Rainbow Brite*, Stephen King, and *Small Wonder*: a show about a robotics engineer who designed a little girl robot named Vicki and tried to pass her off as a member of his family. The comic relief often came from Vicki not being able to assimilate in a functioning human world. And this resonated with me: I had to wear two age hats in order to fit in with the people around me, and I didn't quite wear either very well. And as the years passed, I realized I never felt I'd had permission to just be me.

Mel's story resonated with me too. She's a divorced CEO in her fifties who'd never felt safe to be herself. Who hadn't truly known herself but had made it another full-time job to search for her.

"I feel like I've tried everything," she told me during our consultation. "Coaching, therapy, books, retreats. I know I'm holding something in my body, but I can't figure out what it is. And I don't want to give up on this. *I want to stop being the person who can handle it all.*"

She also wore two different hats. I noticed when she filled out her intake form, she'd used the name Mel, but her Zoom name during our first session read Melinda. As someone who's had her name mispronounced her entire life (it's pronounced REE-nuh, in case you're wondering), I take pride in addressing people correctly.

"Do you go by Mel or Melinda?" I asked. That one simple question ended up revealing the weight she carried.

"I always introduce myself to people as Melinda, and when I say it, it doesn't sound like *me*. Melinda is rewarded in the world. She's revered, impressive. It's the professional me that people find to be unbelievably capable and admirable. It's tiring being her."

"So who is Mel?" I asked.

"Mel is playful. It's who I show up as with the people I love. There's an intimacy to being called Mel, an intimacy I don't share with many people. But she is who I want to be. *I want to feel safe to be fully myself.*"

She'd traveled the journey of personal development and—like me—had fallen short of reaching her aha moment. She yearned for the same type of inner knowing I'd found through my sound bath.

I don't play crystal bowls, but I use techniques with my clients that are designed to accomplish the same thing that happened to me during the sound bath: bringing you to a state where your conscious, thinking brain can take a back seat while your subconscious gets behind the wheel. These techniques—as you'll soon see—allow you to tap into an older, more badass version of yourself.

Like Marie in the last lesson, Mel completed a writing assignment where she detailed what her life would look like if shame *weren't* an option. She said, in part:

I wouldn't waste time ruminating over things—kicking myself for messing up, for saying the wrong thing, for not being flawless. I wouldn't waste my time and energy on that anymore.

I would just be honest in the moment rather than try to hide when I feel like I got something wrong. "Oops, yeah, sorry, I said the wrong thing. What I meant was…"

I would feel closer to (certain) friends because I would more freely tell them that I want/need them. I would also probably let go of some people—stop trying to make them who I wish them to be.

I would speak up for myself when I feel uncomfortable in a situation, with confidence and grace, and without worrying that I might offend someone or that my feelings are not valid.

I would have clearer boundaries and would communicate/exercise those without getting angry. I think the anger comes when I am not clear about my boundaries (or my right to even have boundaries) and so I allow them to be violated and only push back when feeling pushed to the edge.

Without shame, I would feel free. Both held and free.

———

Our brains are like boom boxes with a dual cassette deck: one of those cassettes is the shame cassette. On it, you'll find an infinite (and nasty!) playlist of all the external messages you uncovered in Lesson 2. The goal in this writing assignment is to identify what's currently playing on the shame cassette. For Mel, that tape was saying over and over again, "You're not safe to be you."

I asked Mel to close her eyes, take a deep breath, and feel that feeling: the feeling of shame, of not feeling free to be fully herself.

"Where do you feel that in your body?" I asked.

"It's in my shoulders, my neck, my chest."

"Let your imagination start giving this feeling a shape and a form. What color is it? What texture is it? Is it still or moving?"

"It's an amorphous shape, kind of like a blob. It feels warm, and it's moving. It's a dark brown or burgundy."

"Okay. Now, imagine going *inside* that shape. Feel yourself in there. And tell me: what emotion lives inside there?"

"Sadness. It's sadness."

"Now, sit in that sadness. And as you do, your imagination will bring up a memory of the first time you can remember feeling that sadness. And that memory will just pop in. It may not make any sense at all, but tell me what comes up for you."

"I'm four years old. I struggled with having separation anxiety from my mom. She'd send me to camp, and I would cry constantly and beg for her to pick me up and go home. One day, she brought me to camp, and I walked her around, showing her all the things I'd been working on. She said, 'You seem okay. I can go to work now.' I watched her drive off, and I panicked because I couldn't get her back."

"And what decision did you make about yourself in that moment?"

"My neediness is wrong and too much. I have to figure out a way to suck it up. It's a problem. It's shameful to have strong feelings and experience fear."

"Now, Mel, I want you to imagine you're sitting next to that four-year-old version of you. The one who thinks she can't be scared or have strong feelings. What would you say to her?"

"I would tell her that moms *want* to be there for their kids. It's okay to be scared, and there's nothing to be ashamed of."

"All right. Now, I want you to imagine you're the 80-year-old, most sage, wise, badass version of Mel. Get into *her* head. And once you're there, I want you to imagine 80-year-old Mel sitting next to the current age Mel. What would 80-year-old badass Mel say to the Mel today about her feeling like she's not safe to be herself?"

"She'd say, 'You're smarter than that. You know that you're a badass. People love you even more when you allow yourself to be vulnerable. You're a leader by being vulnerable. You're a role model. Being vulnerable makes you and the people around you happier and freer.'"

Once I brought Mel out of the exercise with some deep breaths, I explained to her that those words from her 80-year-old badass *are* her inner knowing. No coach, therapist, friend—no one—can say those words to a person and have them truly resonate. Your 80-year-old badass—*that is you*. She knows things. It's within your best interests to listen to her.

Mel had done inner child work before, a technique that's extremely common in conventional talk therapy. It's a process where you try to sit and reparent your inner child, giving them the love and care they may have been deprived of.

But what about the person we are today? Aren't we *still* children in some ways? How do we move forward? By harnessing your 80-year-old badass, you're able to essentially perform inner child (er, adult) work in real time, over and over again. "What would your 80-year-old badass say?" is a common response I use when clients ask me for advice. Because that version of you gives very few fucks and always has your back.

As someone who felt the pressure of having to have her shit together all the time, Mel had never been given the space to consider that perhaps there was a part of her that was even smarter and wiser than the woman she is today. And after all the therapy, retreats, and books, she'd finally started cracking the code. She began speaking up at work. She told friends and family how much they truly mean to her.

"Part of me understands the absurdity now of some of the limits I've put on myself. Not only am I safe to be fully myself, it's not even a question on the table. It goes without saying."

We all have our inner unique boom boxes. And it's important to remember: the shame tape is only *one* tape in there. Your 80-year-old badass tape is the other. And in any given moment, you have a choice: which of these do I want to listen to?

Let's start by figuring out what tapes are playing.

The Shame Tape

"But, Rena, I don't *have* a shame tape!" you may be thinking. Because again, shame is a yucky word that a lot of people don't walk around using. But I can almost *guarantee* you have a shame tape, even if it doesn't feel like it. So bear with me and spend some time writing your responses to the following questions:

-   What would my life look like if shame weren't an option?
-   How would I live without fear? Without judgment?

- How would my day-to-day life look different?
- How would my life purpose look different?

Once you've done that, dig deeper and ask: What's the message kicking around in my head right now that's *preventing* me from living my life without shame?

By way of example, here are some brief excerpts from former Shameless clients and the shame tape messages we extrapolated:

> I wouldn't be so defensive in our relationship. When it comes to intimacy, I would be more courageous to speak up about what I like, what I don't like.
>
> **Question:** Why don't I express my preferences or disagree?
>
> **Shame Message:** I have to be a good girl.

> Could I be that badly and scantily dressed girl on the dance floor? Could I be a shameless vixen? Could I ever look relaxed and not uptight in public? Being able to just let go and enjoy life? That sounds nice.
>
> **Question:** Why can't I let loose where other people might be watching?
>
> **Shame Message:** I have to be "age appropriate."

> I would be able to try other types of dating—with women or with couples.
>
> **Question:** Why can't I try new things?
>
> **Shame Message:** I'm not valuable unless I'm an expert at what I'm doing.

You may have one message or several. That's what's on your shame tape.

The 80-Year-Old Badass Tape

You'll now walk yourself through the exercise I performed with Mel earlier.

Start by closing your eyes and repeating the messages(s) you uncovered on your shame tape. Pay close attention to your body. Where does that message live? It could be a feeling. It could even be a tension or a tightness.

And as you focus on that feeling, your imagination will begin to give it a shape and a form. What color is it? What size is it? Is it hollow or solid? Is it still or moving? What temperature is it? Notice as many details as you can.

Keeping your eyes closed, imagine being inside that shape. Look around. This may be a familiar place. It might be a random space. It might be a place you've never seen before. But sense how it feels to be in there. What *emotion* lives in this space?

Once you've identified that emotion, let your imagination bring up a memory of the first time you can remember feeling it. Replay that memory, noticing as many details as you can.

Then ask yourself: What decision did I make about myself or the world at that time (i.e., during the memory you're thinking of)?

Now imagine you're sitting alongside that younger version of you. What would you tell them about the decision they made? How would you soothe them?

And *now* imagine you are the 80-year-old, most sage, wise, badass version of you. Get into that person's head. What would

80-year-old badass you say to the you sitting here today about the shame message(s) and beliefs you have?

Let the wisdom flow. Sit with it. And when it feels complete, bring your awareness back to the room you're in. Take a few deep breaths, and gently open your eyes.

As you move forward in your day-to-day life, as decisions— both big and small—present themselves to you, ask yourself: What would my 80-year-old badass do?

Your brain is a dual cassette boom box, and it's likely that shame tape has been playing at full volume for a loooooong time. So be patient with yourself. Understand that you're now choosing to listen to a much kinder and more powerful tape. In time, it'll become easier to harness that inner knowing. You'll begin to see it as part of your environment, like elevator music playing in the background. You'll begin to see it as you.

Be Too Much

sat in my friend's backyard, a group of close female pals congregating over mimosas, enjoying the spring sun.

"Tomorrow's the big day," I told them. "I'm dyeing my hair pink!"

"Wow! And you're doing it on Easter!" one of them said. "That is so fucking perfect!"

"Why? Because I'm going to look like the Easter bunny?"

"No, girl. *Because it's your fucking resurrection.*"

I'd left the law a mere few months beforehand. In my previous professional life, I wouldn't have been able to have pink hair. Looking outside the norm was a big no-no, especially in the courtroom. I once found out two male public defenders had placed a $100 wager on whether I—a woman who made it a full-time job to pretend to be straitlaced and anything but "sexy" in the workplace—had tattoos.

When a new gym opened up around the corner from my house a decade ago, I walked in after work—in my business suit—to sign up for a membership. I also decided to take advantage of their offer for a free personal training session, and I met the trainer who I'd be coming back to later in the evening. When I returned in my tank top and workout leggings, the actual words that came out of his mouth were "Wow. You look like a different person. When you were here earlier, I thought to myself, 'This woman probably hasn't gotten laid in five years.'"

So yes. This was my resurrection. I went from being the person who wouldn't show her bare arms at work to posting half-naked boudoir photos on social media. I went from being the woman who hid to one who shone. But first I had to stop acting like a chameleon to make other people comfortable.

And I know I'm not the only one who's done this dance. As women, we're taught to not be too loud. Too slutty. Too smart. Too opinionated. *Too much.*

I'm here to help you unlearn much of what you've been taught. To show you the absolute freedom and joy that live somewhere over the shame rainbow. To remind you that modesty isn't a virtue; it's a way of keeping us complacent. And as with most of the other damaging external messages we get, we learn the modesty myth at a very young age.

When I was in fourth grade, my teacher gave the class a Thanksgiving art assignment. She passed out two options: a fall cornucopia and a turkey. Our homework was to pick one, color it in at home, and return it the next day where it would be displayed on our holiday classroom wall.

I chose the turkey, taking care to use alternating brown markers to fill in each small feather. The idea backfired, and it ended up looking like a big brown blob. So I decided to spruce it up by making a colorful frame around it with construction paper.

Which also backfired.

It wouldn't fit on our holiday board. I told my teacher as much. Her response?

"You should've thought about that before you tried to make yours bigger and better than everyone else's."

I can't tell you what I had for dinner last week, but those words are permanently etched into my memory. Do I think my fourth grade teacher permanently fucked me up? No, I won't go that far. But that memory is a bookend in a library full of messages I received throughout my life that reiterated *You are too much*. Or, put another way, *There's something inherently wrong with you*.

Which is exactly what shame is: a feeling that we are flawed and therefore unworthy of love and belonging. Guilt says "I did something bad"; shame says "I *am* bad."

There's an evolutionary reason why we feel shame. As hunters and gatherers, we depended on our closely knit communities for survival, and when there was a threat of being devalued by that community, this unpleasant feeling—that we now understand to be shame—would creep in to keep us in check. We weren't designed to ruffle feathers; we were designed to fit in.

The problem is, we're not hunters and gatherers anymore. And shame is now considered to be a *psychologically damaging* emotion. It's bad for us. If our brains are like computers, when it comes to shame, we're essentially walking around with clunky, outdated desktops that also have a virus on them.

And these messages we receive when we're younger—ones that encourage us to be modest, to stay small, to not be too much—are in themselves viruses that spread and permeate our lives.

My client Carolina had also received messaging about being too much when she was younger. As we were searching for her 80-year-old badass tape, she recounted a memory from when she was nine years old. Back then, she dreamed of becoming a waitress when she got older, and she was presented with an opportunity to realize that dream as a child. Her schoolteacher announced that some visitors from a local retirement home would be coming to the school in a few days for tea (she grew up in England) and that she'd select a few of the students to act as waiters and waitresses for them.

Carolina wasn't picked.

On the day of the tea, she decided to bring along a pair of black pants and a white shirt in case she'd be able to help out.

Instead of thanking her, Carolina's teacher berated her.

"And what decision did you make about yourself on that day?" I asked Carolina.

"I'm bad for going above and beyond," she said.

Even though she was now in her thirties (and working in marketing, not as a waitress), her shame tape still said "I have to blend in. I have to stay invisible."

She wanted to be visible though. She had a closet full of black clothes but wanted to live her life in color. In her own words, she wanted to become confident: the one trait she'd suppressed her entire life.

But what did confidence mean to her?

"I want to be able to walk down the street wearing whatever I like and not have to worry about people thinking I'm ugly...but

also not worry about them thinking *I think I am good-looking.*"
In other words, Carolina didn't want to be perceived as arrogant.

There is a fundamental difference between confidence and arrogance: arrogance is feeling like you're better than everyone else; confidence is feeling like you're enough exactly as you are.

And here's the deal with confidence: no one is born with it. It's not somehow encoded into our DNA. The only way to cultivate confidence is through action: I'm confident when it comes to speaking in public because I've done a lot of it. I have zero confidence when it comes to surfing because I've never even tried it.

Carolina started finding ways to improve at different hobbies and skill sets. She cleared her dating calendar and signed up for intensive Muay Thai training despite having never practiced martial arts before. Within months, she'd competed professionally and won a match.

She wore a colorful floral dress to a friend's wedding...and then to work.

She eventually went to a women-only sex club on her own.

And then she signed up to train as a professional dominatrix.

Once she started trying new things—and appreciated we're all beginners at something—she believed in her ability to improve.

If you wait until you're confident enough to do the big scary thing, you'll be waiting forever. Confidence is the cart; action is the horse.

But even confidence isn't a shield that protects us from insults. From hurtful people. From the grown-up version of the elementary school teacher who berated us.

I was reminded of this recently when I traveled to central Florida to give a TEDx talk on sexual shame at a state college campus. I'd already gathered from virtual meetings with the TEDx committee that they were nervous (massive understatement) to have me there. Central Florida is one of the most conservative parts of the country, and having a woman get up onstage and talk about play parties, faking orgasms, and sexual fantasies was a deviation from their standard speaker lineups. But I'd had one member of the committee—Joe— who'd loved my application and fought hard to win over the rest of the team.

They held a VIP reception for us at the college the night before the event. All the speakers and committee members were present, along with the college president and other higher-ups. As we sat eating our meals banquet style, Barb—the chair of the TEDx committee, who'd expressed reservations about my talk during our meetings leading up to the event—stood up to address the room.

"I want you to meet all the fabulous speakers who'll be getting up onstage tomorrow." She went around, table by table, introducing each speaker by name, giving a brief spiel about their topic, and then expressing enthusiasm and excitement for their presence.

Until she got to me. "This is Rena, and she came here all the way from California! Rena's going to talk about... Hey, Joe? Why don't you tell us all what Rena's going to talk about?"

She'd thrown him under the bus, but he took it in stride. He stood up and hyped me up to the group, highlighting that I'd signed a book deal (yep, for the one you're reading right now!)

and had recently been a guest on the *Savage Lovecast*, one of the biggest sex and relationship podcasts in existence.

"I'm excited for her to share her message with us," he concluded.

As he sat down, Barb took the baton. "Rena, I hope you know Joe is the only reason you're here right now," she said...in front of the entire room.

"Wow, what a fucking bitch," you may be thinking. At least that's what most of my friends say when I get to this part of the story.

In that moment, I could have been pissed off, humiliated. Any range of emotions would've been understandable. Instead, I chose to use this as fuel for a fire in my belly. When I got up onstage the next day, I was the least nervous I'd been in weeks. I reminded myself that I didn't leave my stable career as a lawyer to remain in the status quo. I was here to be the example of a woman who didn't want to live small anymore. A woman who doesn't see being too much as an insult.

So what do you do in this situation? Maybe you fall back on some catchy advice.

"If you're too much for them, they can go find less!"

"Haters gonna hate!"

"Don't let anyone dull your sparkle!"

I'm here to push you beyond these tweet-sized pep talks. The best way to handle the emotions that come along with someone trying to cut you down to size is to appreciate where *they're* coming from.

Back in Lesson 2, you learned how to dissect the external messages you grew up with. One of the questions you asked for each message was "In what way is this person's lens different from mine, such that I can see where their messaging comes from?"

When it comes to confidence, don't take criticism from someone you wouldn't take advice from.

I walk through life assuming two things: first, all of us are getting by as best we can with the tools we have, and second, people aren't *trying* to be assholes. As much as I'd like to write my fourth grade teacher off as a bitch (and track her down and tell her as much), I'm reminded that her lens was valid *to her*. Her language came from somewhere, right? If that's the messaging she was passing down to impressionable kids, I can only imagine what she'd grown up with. I'm guessing Carolina's teacher was also frazzled as she tried to wrangle a three-ring circus of children, hot tea, and geriatric guests. By recognizing that some people have a really shitty emotional toolbox, we can alchemize our feelings of hurt into something more akin to pity: instead of feeling bad for *yourself*, you feel bad for *them*.

When it comes to the TEDx incident, there's some additional context I haven't given you. While I don't know Barb's backstory entirely, I do know she's a deeply religious woman. I know she'd worked at the college for a while and had a reputation to uphold. Her comment probably had very little to do with me and more to do with her wanting to cover her own ass in front of the college president in case there was backlash after my talk. I don't think she was being deliberately cruel; she was tiptoeing across a professional tightrope as best she could.

In other words: when people are assholes, don't take it personally.

When haters are hating, show them some compassion.

"Hold up! Isn't that excusing abuse?" you might be yelling.

Not at all. You're not excusing *anything*. An explanation isn't an excuse. I'm sure you've heard the term *rose-colored glasses* to refer to people who walk around without a care in the world and think the universe is all sunshine and rainbows. Well, there are people who wear crap-colored glasses too. What I'm asking you to do is recognize that the world only looks like crap to these people because of the lenses they're wearing. Lenses that have corroded with a lifetime of negative or contradictory messaging coming *their* way.

"Oh, that's just their crap-colored glasses talking" is a reminder you can adopt when you encounter them without making any excuses for their behavior.

And, on the flip side, there are genuinely sincere people in the world who think you are fabulous and probably tell you so on a regular basis. Take compliments from them.

No, *really* take the compliments.

Just as saying "I'm sorry, but..." isn't a sincere apology, responding to a compliment with "Yeah, but..." isn't accepting a compliment.

Every time you respond to a compliment with the word *but*, you're essentially telling the person who gave you the compliment, "I think you're full of shit."

So just say "Thank you!" instead.

And if a plain old "Thank you!" leaves too much of a pregnant pause in the air, resist the urge to resort to "Yeah, but..." and replace it with some sparkle:

- "Thank you, and it has pockets!" (I have done this more times than I can count!)
- "Thank you! I worked hard for this."
- "Thank you! It was a gift from my mom, and I love it!"

50 Things

All right, we've covered the naysayers and the yay!sayers. What do *you* say about yourself? Most of us would have an easy time writing out a huge list of traits we don't like about ourselves. Things we're *not* good at. All our flaws.

Instead, you're going to put on a pair of rose-colored glasses and start sending compliments your own way!

Sit down and make a list of 50 Things you love, appreciate, and/or admire about yourself. These can be qualities (physical, emotional, or mental), experiences you've had, or challenges you've overcome.

Similar to the 27 Things exercise you completed earlier, it's important you get all the way to 50. Part of the process is pushing past the resistance...even when you feel like you want to throw in the towel!

Once again, I'll share some of what my prior Shameless clients had to say about themselves.

- I got my motorcycle license.
- I'm never afraid to laugh.
- I'm a warrior.
- I have shown strength in leaving several toxic relationships.
- I love cooking.
- I am imperfect.
- I have a deep vocabulary.
- I have a passion for organization.
- I told my family about being sexually molested.
- I was brave enough to live in New York and Paris, far from family and friends.
- I appreciate a good book.

- I am able to have multiple orgasms.
- I went skiing for the first time in twenty-five years this past winter.
- I have chosen sobriety.
- I love the mole on my stomach.
- I always try to see the good in people.
- I am a great public speaker.
- I love being queer and gay!!!
- I don't need to dress up or wear makeup to be beautiful.
- I got my certificate as a diabetes educator.
- I didn't let depression get the best of me after my dad and brother died ten months apart.
- I don't settle for less.
- I love my laugh, snort and all.
- I mentor new attorneys.
- I smile so big my eyes squint.
- My ADHD brain gives me some amazing superpowers.
- I survived a traumatic divorce.
- I have a meditation practice.
- I love the way my butt looks in a good pair of pants.
- I can reach things in high places.
- I am learning to be my own soulmate and best friend.
- I was a junkie and now I'm not.
- I'm an empathetic and caring physician to my patients.
- I'm willing to make tough decisions to show my kids that boundaries are necessary.

Remember: being too much is a badge of honor. Wear it accordingly!

Love Your Body
with the Lights On

can remember the exact day I formed a "relationship" to food.

I was around six years old, and we were living in Cabo San Lucas, a town in Baja California now known equally for its wild spring breaks and luxurious all-inclusive adults-only resorts.

But back in the mid-1980s, it was barely a spot on the map. The roads were largely unpaved. There wasn't a movie theater in town. We didn't even have channels on our TV. This was a far cry from the life I knew as a kid back in LA, full of shopping malls, trips to Disneyland, and McDonald's Happy Meals. I ached for all of them.

But there was one activity here in Cabo I also yearned for that didn't exist back in LA: parasailing. Every day, I'd see humans floating in the sky, suspended by large parachutes. That looked fun as hell, and I wanted in on it.

The problem was, there was a minimum weight requirement. At the time, I was an average height and weight for my age, and that wouldn't do. I'd need to gain about twenty pounds before my airborne dreams could come true. Like a kid hoping and praying she'd be tall enough to meet the little line on the wall to ride the big scary roller coasters, I had a clearly demarcated threshold. But this was a benchmark I had control over. I couldn't will myself to get taller, but I could will (or feed) myself to get heavier.

And so I did.

In my hunt for the perfect caloric bang for buck, I discovered Mamuts: a Mexican sandwich cookie the size of my palm, filled with marshmallow and covered in chocolate. They came individually wrapped in shiny blue foil, a friendly sketch of a woolly mammoth beckoning you to rip through and bite into the combination of textures and flavors. When I needed some variety, Twinkies were also available.

My calorie-rich and nutrient-deficient diet worked perfectly in conjunction with the weight I was already putting on from being a growing little girl. And before long, I found myself strapped into a harness, floating peacefully above the Sea of Cortez.

Once back on land, I started to notice shifts. Adults calling me "*gordita*," assuming from my blond hair I wouldn't understand. Forgetting to bring a swimsuit to a friend's house and being able to fit into her mom's better than I could fit into hers. As an American, I already felt like a stranger in a strange land; as a chubby kid, I felt at once invisible and impossible to ignore.

I could say "I've struggled with my weight my entire life," and you'd probably get the general gist of what I mean. But "struggle" isn't actually what I was doing. As I got older, I discovered it was just as easy for me to lose weight as it was to gain it.

As an adult, I've been as small as a size 2 or as large as a size 14. I did keto before it was even called keto (anyone remember Atkins?). I was on phentermine (a doctor-prescribed diet pill) for a few years. I've been to Weight Watchers meetings. I've counted macros. I've persisted on a diet of booze and french fries for months at a time, giddy at the numbers dropping on the scale.

I haven't "struggled" with my weight; I've been *aware* of it, for better or worse. My weight was a barometer of my mental state. If I was bored or stressed, I'd eat and gain weight. If I was anxious, the thought of food made me sick, and I'd drop weight quickly.

At one point in my midtwenties, I decided there was a threshold called "the five pounds of invisibility" whereby I could predict whether I'd get male attention at bars based on whether my weight exceeded an arbitrary five-pound range. "I'm pushing 140 now, so no one's gonna look twice at me." Talk about a self-fulfilling prophecy.

But even at my "thinnest," I still never felt comfortable being naked in bed with another human if the lights were on. Daytime sex? Shut those curtains and hide me under the sheets. Nighttime? Black as espresso, please. I hated my body when it was bigger, but I didn't actually *love* it at any weight.

When I was in my late thirties, my therapist asked, "What would happen if you stopped weighing yourself every day?"

My mind raced. Was she fucking insane? "Yeah, I don't think that's gonna work for me. People say the best way to actually manage your weight and stay within a healthy range *is* to weigh yourself every day. So this is actually good for me."

"Bullshit. If that were true, you wouldn't have yo-yoed so drastically your entire life, Rena."

Well, no. She didn't actually say that.

She let the matter go and didn't push it. I kept weighing myself as usual, using it as a daily form of either personal validation or self-loathing. The scale was a toxic security blanket, but it was *my* toxic security blanket.

But when I moved out from the home I shared with my husband, the scale stayed with him. I didn't have the mental bandwidth to think about buying furniture, much less a scale.

I started eating intuitively, which is a fancy word for saying I ate what I wanted, when I wanted it. No bingeing (i.e., muting). No counting. No pressure, one way or the other.

Other than trips to the doctor's office, I didn't step on a scale for over a year.

And something magical happened: once I stopped having a relationship *to* my weight, I started having a relationship *with* my body. It wasn't a vessel that was waging war against me. There wasn't the Rena above the neck and the Rena below. I was one fully formed human.

Author Sonya Renee Taylor discusses the idea of "radical self-love" in her book *The Body Is Not an Apology*. And what she means by that is that self-love isn't something we go out and find. As babies, we're born with it. We don't have hang-ups; in fact, we're kind of obsessed with our bodies. Our hands. Our feet.

We came into this world loving our bodies.

And then something happens. For me, it was that motherfucking parasail. But let's be real: it would've been something else. After I'd started living on Lean Cuisines my freshman year of high school to get the singer of a band to like me (it worked), there was always some other reason for me to *not* love the body I lived in.

Sometimes, though, our self loathing stems from factors outside our control, like chronic illness or an accident. My client Ruby, for example, had been dancing for as long as she could remember. Then she suffered an unexpected injury, which left her unable to exercise as much. She put on weight as a result. Once the injury healed, she didn't go back to dancing. Not because she couldn't dance anymore but because she thought she was too big to do it. She even passed up a chance to tour as a backup dancer for Lizzo because of her low body image. She abandoned her lifelong goal of professional dancing for a software position at one of the largest and most prestigious tech companies in the world.

It had been seven years since she'd danced when she came to me. But her relationship with her weight had started long before then.

"Since I was a kid, my dad would say to me, 'If you were thinner, you'd be prettier.'"

Not only did Ruby's relationship to her body affect her professional pursuits, she tied her worth as a partner to the number she saw on a scale.

"I never approached men. I would force myself to like guys who approached me because I truly thought I wasn't 'thin enough' to be picky."

As a result, she got into a five-year relationship with a man who kept her isolated from her friends and perpetuated her belief that no one else would love a woman like her.

It was her ending that relationship with him—and wanting to forge a new relationship with her body—that brought us together.

"So obviously, I'm not a nutrition coach or personal trainer,"

I explained to her during our consultation. "I'm not here to help you 'lose weight.' I'm here to help you love your body as it looks *today*."

As a coach and educator, I've come up with a simple framework to guide people on creating a new and loving relationship with their body: the CAMP method. And it's broken down like this:

- Compassion
- Adoration
- Media Awareness
- Perspective

Compassion

Put simply, talk to yourself like someone you love.

The easiest way to do this is to imagine having a conversation with your best friend. Or daughter. Or niece. Or a small version of you. Pick *one* person who you would absolutely never say anything cruel or critical toward. I call this person your compassionate anchor.

I have twin nieces, and I think of them both together as my compassionate anchor. If I look in the mirror and have something shitty to say about myself, I imagine one of them saying it to me: "Auntie Muzzy, I think I look fat in this." And then I come up with a compassionate response *for myself*.

You wouldn't dare tell your best friend her breasts are too small to wear that top or that no one wants to see her fat rolls hanging over her jeans, would you? So don't say that shit to yourself.

Right now, commit to picking your compassionate anchor (or

anchors, as I did!). Write down the following: "I won't say anything to myself that I wouldn't say to _____." And whenever the nasty self-talk starts, honor the promise you've made to yourself.

Adoration

If I told you to stand in front of a mirror and write down all the things you see that you don't like, you'd probably have an easy time with it. (Do not do that!) You've probably been doing this inadvertently anyway. Our goal here is to undo the critical gaze and replace it with an adoring one.

Instead, I'll assign you the task I assign all my clients: look in the mirror nude once per day for a week and write down one thing you see that you like. You can borrow from the 50 Things you recorded liking about yourself in Lesson 6 if you're stumped, but don't miss this opportunity to love something about yourself, *in the moment*.

I'll admit, for some clients, this is in fact the most difficult assignment they complete. Here are examples of their unique backgrounds and experiences:

- Client Ana said, "Rena, by the time I reached day seven, I was scraping the bottom of the barrel. 'I guess I have nice cuticle beds?'"
- Rachel was teased for her slim frame and small breasts growing up and asked if she was a member of the "itty-bitty titty committee" in elementary school. (Kids can be cruel.)
- Carolina was *convinced* she had a "pretty fit body but an ugly face."

- Mel could only see her sagging skin, a reminder of the fact that she was getting older.
- The stretch marks on Marissa's stomach convinced her she'd never feel sexy again after having kids.
- Farrah couldn't even bear to look at her face in the mirror for extended periods of time, much less her entire naked body. So instead, she gradually began undressing day by day, focusing first on her face, then eventually moving down and focusing her attention to one zone of her body at a time.

If you're hung up on your flaws too, figure out the part (or parts) of your body that troubles you most. Then use your week to gently lean into admiring it. This will be hard at first—you're undoing perhaps a lifetime's worth of negative self-talk—but over time, you'll create new neural pathways and change your lens from one of critique to one of adoration.

Maybe you can't go from hating your stretch marks to loving them in a single attempt. The first step can be simply *neutralizing* how you feel about them. This can be a simple statement of fact (no judgment allowed), like "I have stretch marks." Eventually, push yourself to think of the ways your stretch marks *are* beautiful. This can look like "My stretch marks are a reminder of how my body made space for me to carry my baby."

Media Awareness

Think of how many industries would collapse if we started loving our bodies tomorrow. No, seriously. Take a few minutes and think about that.

Mainstream consumer culture is *built* on us having antagonistic relationships with our bodies. Because if we felt enough just as we are, we wouldn't need to buy much, would we?

"Media makes women feel like shit about themselves" is knowledge as common as cigarettes being bad for you. But most of us have a hell of a lot more understanding about why cigarettes are bad for us than why media is damaging. Billboards, secondhand smoke ads, photos of cancerous lungs—the negative consequences of smoking have been spread far and wide. Which is why I'm about to share some body-image research with you.

A study was done in Fiji, where the robust (i.e., rounded, not skinny) form has been celebrated among women for a very, very long time. In the nineties, a Harvard researcher took a look to see what effect three years of American TV (soap operas, *Beverly Hills 90210*, etc.) had on young women. The results were staggering. Within a three-year period, eating disorders among young teenage girls more than doubled. Seventy-four percent said that they felt too big or too fat. *In three years, Western media was able to rewrite what was considered beautiful in that culture.*

If you don't think your media exposure is affecting how you think about your body, *think again.*

So is the solution to crawl in a hole and completely unplug from the outside world? No, obviously. We just needed to change the channel.

It used to be we had one remote control: the one to our TV. But now? Our phones are our remote controls to the entire fucking universe. And we forget that—just as with our TV remote—we can choose what channel to watch. We get to choose the news and TV shows we consume. What Instagram accounts we follow.

The YouTube tutorials we pore over. The TikTok videos we binge. So as you're consuming all those, ask yourself: does this make me feel better or worse about my body? From there, start purging.

"But, Rena, does that mean I need to totally delete [Instagram, or whatever app makes you feel like shit]?" Not at all. You can purge the toxic garbage and *replace* it with messages that make you feel good. There are so many wonderful body-positive accounts out there now. Search for them!

Same goes for porn, which I'll be discussing more in Lesson 21, "Make Porn Your Friend."

Take some time right now and go through your social media. Any account that makes you feel bad about yourself? Unfollow. Unsubscribe. (Or if it's a friend, then "mute" seeing their posts.) Remove any content that will tempt you to start talking negatively to yourself. You might eventually go back and engage with their accounts down the road, but right now, set yourself up for success on your journey to loving your body.

Perspective

I grew up in Los Angeles. Other than my four-year childhood stint in Cabo and a few years away for college, I've spent my entire life in a city known for being full of (conventionally) "beautiful people." Most of the fitness instructors I've ever had have been aspiring models and actors. Some cities have Mary Kay parties; LA has Botox parties.

It's when I travel to places like the Midwest that I realize how much of my perspective on beauty has been shaped by the world I'm walking into every day. A world where I don't quite fit the bodily ideal. But as a native Angeleno, I also see so, so clearly: there is very little correlation between what you look like and how confident you are.

Say what?

Yes. In my personal experience (admittedly anecdotal, not scientific), the most confident women I've known haven't conformed to standard American ideals of beauty.

Confidence is sexy. Think about the best sexual lovers you've ever had. Yes, stop and think.

Now ask yourself: did any of them have "perfect" bodies?

I'm gonna guess the answer is no. But did any of them shy away from being seen? Because how sexy is it to see someone in their own skin? Owning their body exactly the way it is.

Think of someone you've been with who doesn't fit the stereotype of "ideal" beauty in terms of body. How did their relationship with their own body affect your attraction to them? It's all about perspective. You can go to the gym every day of the week. You can get all the cosmetic surgery you want. But you can't buy confidence.

As we discussed in the previous lesson, confidence comes from action: *you become confident by doing the damned thing.*

Remember my client Ruby, the dancer? She pushed outside her comfort zone and signed up for a two-day dance intensive with a choreographer she admires.

"I'd wanted to do it for years, but I kept telling myself I was too overweight, my body was too injured." And she proved herself wrong. And in proving herself wrong, she kept going. By the time we finished working together, she hadn't shed a single pound, but for the first time in her life, she said, "I'm beautiful. I'm hot."

A year later, she's dancing more than she ever has before.

And what's more, she confessed a crush to a friend she'd liked for years. She went from being the person who would never put herself out there to doing the big scary thing. And they're now in the most healthy and loving relationship she's ever had.

Think of what your big scary thing is. And do it.

The mere *idea* of loving your body may seem like the biggest, scariest thing of them all, considering we live in a society that benefits from our antagonistic relationships with our bodies. Start CAMPing your way into rebellion, one day at a time.

Turn Yourself On

t was a Friday night in December, chilly outside (as chilly as it can be in Los Angeles during winter). I sat cozily on my couch in a blue bathrobe, my cat cuddling and purring beside me. And that was where I wanted to stay.

"I'm supposed to go to a women's sex party tonight," I DMed a colleague of mine. "But all I want to do is be a grandma and stay home with my cat."

After making jokes that she and her wife typically go to bed at the exact time I was looking to start my night, she offered me some encouragement. "Change your mood. Change your mindset."

So I pulled off my robe and slipped into a strappy black lingerie set. And as I did that, I imagined what the other women would be wearing. Would they also offer hints of their lingerie poking out from under their low-cut dresses? Would the tops of garters reveal themselves suggestively as they sat cross-legged on the sofa?

And sure enough, that was what I needed to get up and moving. Of course I hadn't felt sexy lounging in my blue bathrobe, an accoutrement so indicative of a lazy state of mine that my ex-husband would tease, "Oh fuck. It's blue bathrobe time!" when I'd retreat into our TV room, knitting supplies in hand.

I felt like a grandma because I was acting like one.

There's a scene in the movie *Bad Moms* where Mila Kunis's character removes her T-shirt in front of her friends—friends who are trying to get her dressed up for a wild night out. She reveals a beige full-coverage bra, which one of her (horrified) friends dubs a "mom bra."

"This isn't my mom bra," she snaps back. "This is my sexy bra."

I knew that bra well. My drawer used to be filled with them. Full coverage, flattening my 36C breasts so that I wouldn't have buttons gaping as I stood in court trying to be anything but sexual. Trying to get juries to like me and female judges not to see me as a threat.

I had desexualized myself, so it made sense that I felt superbly unsexy.

So often, we're waiting for some external validation to tell us we're sexy. (Like, literally, another human to say to us, "You're so sexy.") But our own sense of desire has to come from within. We can't expect to turn on—or be turned on by—another person unless we know how to turn ourselves on.

In the last lesson, you learned how to love your body with the lights on. But how do you *desire* your body?

If you're someone who falls into the "mom bra" category (even if, like me, you're not a mom), I offer you a challenge: go through your underwear drawer *right now* and get rid of anything you wouldn't want a sexual partner to see you in. Yes, I'm serious. If it's not good enough for them, it sure as hell isn't good enough for you.

And what do you replace it with? With whatever makes *you* feel sexy. There's no one-size-fits-all for this. I don't feel sexy in anything that doesn't support my breasts. No underwire? No thanks. I'd look and feel better in a sports bra. Some thigh-high sweater socks? Sign me the fuck up.

You're allowed to define "sexy" however you choose to. And if you have no idea where to begin, start by starting. Go to a store and try a bunch of items on, even if they feel very much outside your comfort zone. And if you can't get to a store (or your local ones are stocked with nothing but mom bras), look for an online retailer with a generous return policy.

When I realized the power of buying lingerie that made me feel sexy, I initially fell into what I call the black trap: I wound up with a drawer full of black lacy and strappy items. And what helped me get out of the black trap was allowing someone else to send me some color. For the last few years, I've used a monthly service that styles a box of lingerie for me. They send me a box, and I pick what I want and send back the rest. As a result, I have a rainbow assortment of colors and styles that I never would have pulled off the rack. (I also loathe shopping, so this has been a huge help.)

Am I telling you you need to go into debt stocking your drawers with La Perla and Agent Provocateur? Absolutely not. I don't currently own any designer lingerie, and I don't expect you to (but have at it if you can afford it!). However, even if it's one piece—one bra, one set of panties—start somewhere.

Once you've found an outfit that makes you *feel* sexy, it's time to shift your erotic gaze. The best way I've found to do this is through photography.

All my clients are assigned the task of taking an erotic photo. It doesn't need to be in-your-face and graphic; it only needs to capture *you* through an erotic gaze. I don't require them to share the photo with me (though a few of them have), but I do ask them to describe what the experience was like for them:

————

Empowering. It felt good and sexy, and I walked away holding my head higher. At first, I thought, "Oh, you kind of look like a fool," but then I just brushed that off and got comfortable and decided to love myself the way I am and own myself.

————

I tried my hand at the pentagram harness from a shibari YouTube video. It took me a little bit, but I got the steps down. I then tried several shots of the harness with my head out of the frame. That was successful! I thought it looked cool. I then decided to switch the filter to black and white. That was the ticket for me! In the end, I was very pleased with the erotic photo of myself, and I let go of perfectionism to pick my best photo option.

————

I was actually really dreading this, but I got a new haircut and decided to get ready for the day and go for it. I took a few and did a bunch of different things just accentuating my boobs still in a tank and bra but pulling the tank down a bit to show the bra and let one nipple just peek out to play.

I took a few pictures in black and white wearing a black lace bra and thong. The photo I liked the most of the session is the one where I am lying down sideways in bed, and the camera is on my back. The picture is taken from an angle where you see my butt first, then my back and my face looking toward my back to the camera. The main focus is on my butt and hips. I felt sexy taking this photo. I actually can't believe how good the photos look and how simple it was to do this photo shoot.

I had a boudoir session last year (almost exactly a year ago) and loved it. This past weekend, I pulled out a few of the pieces I'd purchased, grabbed a set of stockings, heels, and a silk robe, and created a few shots where I tied my wrists behind me with velvet ribbon. I took a few shots where the outline of my breasts showed and let my nipples peek through. I felt powerful, sexy, and desirable looking at those shots and have started planning a second shoot for next year as well.

A boudoir photography session, like the one mentioned in that last example, involves hiring a photographer to document you wearing lingerie (or anything that makes you feel sexy). The shots are typically taken in a boudoir (which literally just means "bedroom" in French) and are sexually suggestive without being pornographic. (If you still have no idea what I mean, google "boudoir photography" and take a look!)

I can't recommend boudoir sessions enough. Yes, a lot of women will sit for one as a gift (wedding, anniversary, etc.) for their partner, but I've worked with several single clients who found the experience to be one of the most empowering things they've ever done.

One client, Laura, was kind enough to share her professional boudoir photos with me. A few of them featured her in the type of lingerie you'd typically think of as "sexy": black lace, garter belts. But she also had a series of her sporting a T-shirt from one of her favorite punk bands, boy briefs peeking out underneath, striped knee-high socks suggestively drawing the viewer's eye upward.

I loved her photos because they were multifaceted and showed the different sides of her sexuality: sultry and moody, playful and edgy. They were uniquely her and only *for* her. She'd never done anything like this before, and she decided she wanted to make it a yearly gift to herself.

I've also worked with women who are no strangers to posing half-nude in front of cameras. Models and actors. Women who use OnlyFans as a side hustle for some extra spending money. And women who simply enjoy sending nudes to people they're sexually involved with.

"This is the first time I've ever taken these photos *for me*," most of them say. It's a way for them to reclaim their sexuality, a reminder that they own it and are merely leasing it out to others.

Just as every woman's idea of "sexy" varies, there's a huge spectrum of touch that turns us on. But once again, we rely often on other people to teach us about our arousal. We wait to be touched to learn what feels good.

And I'm not talking about masturbation here (yet). I'm talking about G-rated touching.

Back in the 1960s, sexual pioneers William Masters and Virginia Johnson developed a therapeutic technique called sensate focus. Sensate focus was designed as a series of touching exercises to help couples "let go of their expectations and judgements of mutual touching, and instead focus solely on the sensory aspects of touch like temperature, texture, and pressure." The practice is still widely used by sex therapists today (which is saying a lot, considering it's about sixty years old). In essence, sensate focus starts with couples touching each other in a very nonsexual way and giving the other feedback on what feels good to them. The practice eventually builds up to gradual sexual touching in subsequent sessions.

I've adapted the Masters and Johnson sensate focus exercise for solo use, and I guide my clients through the G-rated (i.e., nonsexual touching) version of the exercise. Cameras off, I ask them to strip down to bra and underwear (or nude, if they're comfortable with it) and explore different zones of their bodies.

"The goal here isn't to give yourself a massage," I tell them. "The goal here is to figure out what kind of sensation, pressure, and touch feels good to you and where it feels good."

Having conducted this exercise with over one hundred women at this point, I can tell you two things: first, most of us have never mindfully touched our bodies, and second, no two women want to be touched the same way.

Sure, most of us masturbate. We also wipe ourselves when we use the restroom or slather lotion on our bodies, totally on autopilot. But have you ever set aside time to lie down, close your eyes, and touch different parts of your body?

Now's the time.

Sensate Focus

Start by stripping down, giving yourself access to as much skin as possible. Dim the lights or whatever else you need to do to get fully relaxed. Lie down comfortably, and have your phone nearby with a timer set for four minutes.

For the first four minutes, use your hands to explore everything from your collarbone up: your neck, face, ears, scalp. What type of sensation, pressure, and touch do you like?

Once the alarm goes off, set it again for four minutes. Start at your collarbone, but this time, move down your arms to your hands and fingers. What feels good to you?

On the next four-minute round, focus on your torso: your chest, your stomach, and—if it would feel comfortable—roll onto your belly so you can access your back too. What do you like? What do you not like?

Lastly, you'll spend four minutes getting curious about your legs, starting at your hips and working your way down your thighs, knees, calves, and ultimately your feet and toes. Again, take note of what is pleasurable.

Once the timer goes off, write down your observations so

you don't forget them. After my clients complete the exercise with me, I ask them to report back on their findings, which I take note of. Here are a few:

_____

I like touch on the back of my thighs with more pressure so it isn't as ticklish. I like a softer touch on my feet.

_____

The face is a place I don't think about that much. Touching it was quite emotional. On top, I don't like anything sudden or quick. All very slow and wringing inward. I like stroking and tickling. On my legs, tickling didn't feel as nice or connected. I wanted it to be more solid and hard. The leg touching was less emotionally bound or tied. It felt less intimate.

_____

I enjoy holding a hand to my cheek or chest.

_____

Usually foreplay starts with massage (firm touch), but I actually respond most to light, feathery, ticklish touch. I do like that feeling, I just have to be ready for it or else it doesn't feel good.

_____

It feels good to be lightly touched…and it feels good to be smacked!

———

Both sides of my body aren't necessarily the same. The upper inner thigh on the left is more sensitive than the right. I enjoyed feeling touch more to my upper arm than lower arm.

———

Your current or future partner doesn't have a crystal ball. In all likelihood, they're touching you how *they* like to be touched or how a prior partner enjoyed it. It's up to you to use your words and express what type of pressure, sensation, and touch you like.

It's also up to you to describe what type of X-rated touch you like. And—again—the best way to figure that out is on your own.

After you've finished the nonsexual sensate focus, you'll complete the erotic version. Again, strip down and get comfortable. Set a timer for fifteen minutes. This time, though, you're encouraged to incorporate genitals and erogenous zones. And as you do that, imagine there's an imaginary partner there, and practice saying *out loud* what it is you're responding to, like this:

- I like my nipples squeezed hard.
- It feels good when you draw your hand from my neck down to my pussy.
- I love it when you cup my ass like that.

You get the drift.

Will this feel ridiculous and a bit silly? Probably. But if you want to get comfortable telling another person what turns you on, the best place to start is by saying it out loud when you're alone.

When the fifteen-minute timer goes off, then—and only then—are you encouraged to reach orgasm, if you want to, using your hand or whatever toys you normally bring into the mix. So many of us treat masturbation like a wham-bam-thank-you-ma'am and don't spend time turning ourselves on in the process. Here's your chance to get curious about what type of touch you like before you start chasing an orgasm.

The secret to unlocking your sexuality is realizing the key is in *your* hand. It doesn't belong to your partner or your ex or the random person you matched with on a dating app. Start gently turning that key, and a whole new world will open up to you.

9

Fall in Love with Yourself

I sat in Department 30 in the downtown Superior Court, which also happens to be one of the busiest courtrooms in North America. I punched "Flights LAX to Copenhagen" into the outdated Dell desktop staring me in the face, as I'd done many times before.

In the months leading up to my divorce, I'd made it a hobby to pester my then husband to go with me to Copenhagen. I was relentless, like a Midwestern kid bugging her parents to take her to Disneyland. Except logistically, there was no reason we couldn't go. We had the vacation time and a shitload of airline miles.

"I'd rather go somewhere else" was the beginning and end of the conversation each time.

But this day in Department 30 was different. I still had the vacation time. I still had the miles. But the husband was out of the picture.

As I went to click "purchase tickets," a feeling crept in. *Rena, you can't just book a ticket to fly to Europe alone. Ask permission. Always ask permission.*

But I was tired of asking permission. I'd dropped a bomb in my life to *not* have to ask for permission. So I pilfered a huge chunk of my coveted airline miles and booked a business-class ticket to Denmark.

Once there, I read *The Ethical Slut* while sipping cocktails in a smoky cabaret speakeasy. I got lost on city buses. I made friends at a local candlelit bar during Paul Simon night. But it was day three when everything clicked for me. I was on a train headed to an art space on Denmark's coast. I gazed out the train window and began silently sobbing.

An observer might have assumed I was heartbroken. *Poor girl listening to sad music on her headphones. Probably just got dumped by her boyfriend.*

"I love myself," I was thinking, for the first time in my entire life.

Sure, I'd *tolerated* myself before. On long solo drives. During the occasional movie I'd go to, accompanied only by a massive bucket of popcorn. Hell, sometimes I'd even *liked* myself. But that normally happened when other people were there, acting as my mirrors, validating me. Telling me I'm pretty. Or smart. Or funny.

But this was different. Yes, I was single, but not in a state of limbo, waiting for my next love to come along. I had found her. I was her. I am her.

That night, I treated myself to a fancy meal. Afterward, I went to one of Copenhagen's only experimental cocktail bars and spent $30 on a truffle-infused libation. It was absolutely foul and undrinkable, but that wasn't the point. The point was I didn't have to wait for someone to treat me. I was worthy of nice things. I was worthy of wooing. And I've continued wooing myself ever since.

You can love yourself.

And when the moment hits—as it hit me during a winter train ride through Scandinavia—you'll damn well know it. As you'll soon see, you don't need to spend copious amounts of money (or airline miles) to do it, either.

It's not uncommon for clients to have major life events happen during the Shameless program. Unexpected pregnancies. Separations. Deaths. Job-related relocations overseas.

"Life doesn't stop while you're doing the work," I tell them. We make adjustments and pivots as necessary.

With Maria, it was different. During our initial consultation, she was in a serious relationship, and she enrolled in Shameless to work on exploring sexual novelty with her partner. By the time we had our first session a week later, though, she was single. "We broke up because he found out I was cheating on him," she confessed.

It was time to change course.

Instead of focusing on her outward relationship, Maria's new goal was to love herself first. In her words, she wanted to "have happiness from within rather than trying to seek external validation."

And that validation, historically, had come from sleeping with men. She poured sex into a bucket, not knowing the bucket had no bottom. Forever thirsty. Forever dissatisfied.

She'd already been in weekly therapy for a year at that point. Our job wasn't just to discuss where the bottom fell out in the first place but to repair it and make it ironclad moving forward.

As with all my one-on-one clients, Maria crafted an affirmation to serve as an anchor of where she wanted to be at the conclusion of our work together: *I am a fun, courageous, strong, and honest woman who is a good person worthy of endless love.*

"I don't believe a single word of that," she said.

"Exactly," I responded. "If you already believed it, your brain would have nothing to chew on. This is fuel. This is our work."

It was my turn to confess. "To say I know where you're coming from is an understatement. But I'm here to tell you: you can—and will—fill that bucket yourself. If I can do it, anyone can."

Maria lives in a major metropolitan U.S. city. She's bubbly and fun and magnetic. She had no shortage of friends (and suitors) who could fill every minute of her waking life with their company. And fill it they did.

But about halfway through our work together, she started turning inward: watching movies alone, taking erotic photos ("Just for me this time."), cooking herself elaborate meals. One of those meals was pozole. Her late mother cooked it for her growing up, as had one of Maria's ex-boyfriend of hers.

"It's what people who love me cook for me," she said. "I've never made it for myself, though."

Maria sourced an authentic recipe and found fresh herbs to include in it. She documented the lengthy cooking process on her Instagram stories, pork simmering into the early morning hours. She cut no corners. She spared no expense. She harnessed her love into a dish that could have fed over a dozen adults but that was designed for one and only one.

During our final session, I read her affirmation to her again: *I am a fun, courageous, strong, and honest woman who is a good person worthy of endless love.*

"I truly believe it. It's wild that I used to question it."

The first step in falling in love with yourself is the same as falling in love with a partner: courting.

Yes. Start by taking yourself out on a date.

If you're single and unafraid to fly solo, this may sound pretty simple. "I do stuff on my own *all the time*."

But spending time alone is different from taking yourself out on a date. What's the thing you normally *wouldn't* do on your own but would *absolutely* do without question if you were planning a date for someone? You'd probably get out of your sweatpants. You might throw on some makeup. You'd likely map out a charming itinerary.

If you're partnered, this might feel silly. "Wait, so I'm going to leave my significant other at home?"

Yes. Yes, you are.

This doesn't need to cost a ton of money. The magic ingredient is pushing outside your comfort zone and doing something *new*.

There is no recipe for this. And that's the whole point. You—your wants, needs, and desires—are unique. There is no standard script for what will make you feel special. So turn inward and ask yourself: What is my perfect date? What will make me feel alive? What are some small ways I can treat myself? Get the date on your calendar ASAP!

Here are some dates Shameless clients have treated themselves to:

———

I watched the sun rise and then baked homemade biscuits (one of my favorite things to do is bake). I've not baked since my dad passed, early March, and it felt therapeutic. My soul breathed this weekend. I got my nails done Saturday evening and went to a local brewhouse for a burger and beer and ate outside in the fresh air. I slept well Saturday night and got up early Sunday and took off to San Francisco. I walked the wharf and ate my way around the city, enjoying beer and seafood that only I enjoy (nobody in my family likes seafood). It was a beautifully restful time for my mind. I got plenty of fresh air and exercise and got to feel free for the first time in ages. I did what I wanted, when I wanted, and didn't have to worry about how long I was taking or what shops or stores I looked in. It was much needed. I also spent some time creatively thinking about the tattoos that I want and have put off for years and have a consultation booked!!!

———

I have no problem treating myself. I didn't want to just do what comes easy to me and take myself out to dinner. I knew it had to be outdoors, adventurous, and spontaneous, so I decided to up the ante and hike to a clothing-optional hot spring I'd never been to before. I got into my birthday suit and enjoyed the serenity and beauty of the place. I moved about between different tubs and just absolutely allowed myself to be in my body. I realized it's not just about taking myself out to dinner or doing whatever I want. I found that I can give myself the intense pleasures I so enjoy. I thought I needed an adventure buddy/partner—which is nice—but until I meet that person, the world is my playground!! All in all, I feel a profound trust in myself, that I am for the first time loving myself.

———

I got dressed up, put on some glitter and hair extensions, and went to the riverfront where I danced at a silent disco rave for four hours. Before COVID, dancing at shows and events used to be my thing, but I didn't feel like I could do it much solo because I was partnered. I felt obligated to either bring them with me or felt guilty if I went alone or with friends without them. I turned down so many invites because of this. There is nothing holding me back this time. I looked super hot and felt confident moving my body, so it was nice to be seen and see others all dressed up and hot too! I feel like life is returning to me again.

———

Leaving my phone at home was the start to an ideal date. This truly allowed me to disconnect from everything. It amazes me how many times I look for my phone when I'm bored or feeling awkward in public. Eating sushi is something that I usually enjoy with my kids, but this time alone, I was free to order what I like, not worrying about pleasing anyone but myself. Taking myself shopping was fun. Allowing myself the time to pick up and imagine. All the clothes, decor, and beauty items I never have time to look at or shop for. Finally I sat for a mani-pedi, which I rarely allow time or money for. Without my phone, I found myself actually talking to my manicurist. I can't say that

I've ever done that before. I learned so much from this young Vietnamese man, as he explained that his home city just got a Starbucks and KFC for the first time and how there was at least an hour wait to order. Things we take for granted here but also how similar Hawaii is in the fact that we don't have all the chain restaurants and stores. I remembered how exciting it was to stand in line to get into the T. J. Maxx when it opened here. Every time I'm caught admiring my hands and feet, I'm in love with me.

––––––

I got out early on Saturday morning for a walk to a day spa for a full-body massage. Next, I strolled along the park and watched some doggos go for their morning walk near the pond as I made my way to a new coffee shop where I treated myself to a chocolate croissant and a mocha. I savored every bite and sip as I people watched from the sidewalk patio where I sat, momentarily. I contemplated where my feet would take me next...the public library or to an independent bookstore I'd been eyeing for weeks every time I'd go out on a grocery run with my partner. The bibliophile in me felt like I deserved to treat myself to a new book or two. I got to the store and spent a good hour admiring their collection of books and records. I got lost in a title called *The Girl and the Goddess*, which made its way home in my backpack, along with a book on BDSM fantasies and erotica for couples that I thought my partner and I could enjoy together. It felt amazing to get out of the apartment and take myself out to do some of the things that I love to do but usually don't make time to do on my own. What was even more satisfying was being able to forget about the time and just enjoy my thoughts and my own company for a few hours in a totally playful and leisurely way that made me feel good about myself and my passions.

———

Just as there's no limit to how you can express love to others, there are countless ways for you to harness that love and direct it right back at the most important person in your life: you. And once you do, magic happens. If you're single, your standards are higher. Your boundaries are firmer. You're not looking for a person to complete your life (because it's full!) but someone to add sprinkles on top of it. Or, as a client of mine once said, "I'm not settling for crumbs. I want the whole damned cake."

If you're in a relationship, that magic appears differently. Your partner can embrace your newly minted self-love and your recently discovered pleasures and insights. They will be eager to explore with you! It could also mean taking some much-needed "you" time—time away from your family—as a reminder that you have an identity outside your role as mother. Because isn't self-love one of the best lessons you can model for your kids?

So go on. Fall wildly, passionately, unapologetically in love with yourself.

PART 2

PLAY WELL WITH OTHERS

10

Find Your People

was (virtually) face-to-face with one of my heroes.

Dan Savage had invited me to be a guest on *Savage Lovecast*, his renowned podcast that offers no-holds-barred advice on sex and relationships. As we wrapped up our conversation about using BDSM as a healing modality and waited for the green light that our recording had safely downloaded, I had a confession to make.

"I have to thank you, Dan. If it weren't for you—and your podcast—I wouldn't be helping women the way I am today."

He didn't know his voice had kept me company on my daily commute into downtown Los Angeles, a drive that culminated in being surrounded by hundreds of people per day in a chaotic courtroom. People who greeted me on a first-name basis but had no idea who I really was.

I'd discovered his podcast late in the game and made my way through years of archived episodes. I heard from poly folks and kinky folks. Queer and straight and every sexual orientation on the spectrum, including ones I'd never heard of. And it was in those countless hours that I realized: my people are out there. I just needed to find them.

As Brené Brown says, "If we can share our story with someone who responds with empathy and understanding, shame can't survive." When we're in an echo chamber, we can't hear any other music.

And Dan's voice was my siren song. Sometimes it played softly in the background, elevator music to the voices of folks who talked about swingers like they were some sort of freak show. And sometimes, it would be part of a symphony. Like the night I went out to a literary event whose theme happened to be sex positivity. I heard slam poetry from a bisexual woman as I sat next to my then husband. This was the first (and last) time I was at an event with him where sex was discussed positively. Where one man and one woman wasn't the default setting. *My people are out there.*

After the reading, we went for old fashioneds and buffalo cauliflower at a gastropub across the street with some writers we knew. "Well, tonight was an interesting one, huh?" one of them said smugly. The others laughed. I didn't. In under an hour's time, I'd gone from feeling like I was (finally, maybe?) in my element to being sucked right back down to earth. But I'd gotten a glimpse of an entire universe out there, waiting for me.

When I left my marriage a few months later, I was committed to moving beyond the airwaves. Dan's podcast had brought me solace long enough. I needed to find a community of people like me out in the real world.

Which was how I ended up in a conference room at the top of the second tallest skyscraper in Los Angeles. As people a few floors above us ate overpriced meals and enjoyed the unparalleled views of downtown, I was surrounded by a dozen thirty-somethings in a therapeutic polyamory processing group.

Our leader—a well-known and in-demand poly therapist—entered and broke the ice with "So what brings you all here today?"

She gestured at me. "I just left my husband because I realized I'm not wired for monogamy and he is. I want to meet other people who feel the same way."

As she continued around the room, I realized how naive and overly optimistic I'd been.

"I keep trying to be better at poly, but every time he"—the speaker gestured to her long-haired partner—"goes out on a date, I freak out, and I get jealous, and I just want to be better at this whole thing."

"I keep dating women and being up front with them about the fact that I'm poly, and they act like they're fine with it, then they try to 'change my mind.'"

"I have a dream of us being in a relationship with a woman who will act as the mother of our child," one lady recounted. "I want all of us to live under one roof as a family. But we keep getting into arguments about what type of woman we want and have no idea how to even find her."

I didn't want to be beholden to anyone. I didn't want more rules. I wanted fewer. I didn't want to live happily ever after *without* children, much less with them.

Nope. These weren't my people either.

Back at square one.

I started dating, very organically. I reconnected with a few people I'd been romantically involved with before I had a ring on my finger. I indulged a few threads of chemistry I'd felt with men I'd considered to be friends. I was up front with all of them and explained I wasn't looking for monogamy. I described myself as "solo poly" at the time. Many polyamorous arrangements are considered hierarchical—where a "primary" partner or partners serve as "home base" among other "secondary" relationships. At this stage, I was in a primary relationship with *myself*, and *any* other relationships were secondary. My autonomy was paramount, and I wasn't looking to fuse my life with anyone else's through using the "boyfriend/girlfriend" label or moving in together.

Most of my lovers were fine with the arrangement, for their own reasons. One was in an open relationship with their own primary partner. Another was so engrossed in his demanding career that he didn't want a primary partner to begin with. The others just went along with the program, happy to have a woman in their lives who they could drink and have enlightening conversation with and occasionally fuck without any of the demands that come along with the traditional relationship trajectory.

It worked perfectly for me.

I didn't kid myself into thinking I'd find someone exactly like me. My lovers and I were making our way through the same relationship buffet, putting what we wanted on our plates and passing on what we didn't.

Until I met him.

I was at a dive bar in Big Bear, a mountain town a few hours outside LA, with a dozen of my closest, rowdiest friends celebrating my birthday. We'd been on a twelve-hour bender that began with mimosas in our hot tub in the morning and eventually led to a debaucherous night at the local Oktoberfest where a line of strangers formed to give me birthday spankings.

I was ready to call it a night.

"You can't leave now!" my sister pleaded. She'd put in a lot of effort to make the weekend special for me, down to the "It's My Birthday, Bitch!" sash she'd insisted I wear for all the festivities.

"One drink," I conceded.

Our loud (and drunk) crew made its way into the packed, cash-only bar, several residual Oktoberfest hangers-on following us like lost puppies.

A friend of mine and I wrapped a round of foosball with some guys at least a decade our juniors when the tall and handsome man approached me.

"Can I buy you a drink?"

"Which one of my friends sent you over?" I yelled.

"No one sent me over."

"Oh, are you gay?!" (Can you tell I don't get hit on often by strangers at bars?)

"Um, no, I'm not gay. It's your birthday," he said, gesturing at my sash, "and I thought I'd buy the birthday girl a drink."

With the sponsored bourbon rocks in hand, I asked where he was from, fully expecting him to be some local townie who'd smelled fresh meat the second my crew had stumbled in the door.

"I live in Echo Park," he said, a neighborhood of LA that happened to be about a mile from the one I called home at the time.

That one drink turned into more.

"Just so you know, I'm going through a divorce right now and am not looking for conventional monogamy. I'm basically solo poly," I said honestly but with every intention of scaring off this person who I thought was too good-looking to hit on me at a bar.

"Yeah, I've pretty much been solo poly for most of the last decade," he said, proving me wrong yet again.

As our conversation continued—at the bar and later during our dates in LA—I realized this man wasn't approaching the buffet with me. We were in the kitchen, developing our own recipe. One where two people can love each other deeply as primary partners while still maintaining their freedom. A relationship where people can play together or separately. A partnership where there's safety and security coupled with passion and excitement.

More than five years later, and we're still cooking in the kitchen. But we're pretty far from being exactly alike. I don't share his passion for video games. He tolerates my affinity for dark and depressing foreign films. But when it comes to what we want— and *don't* want—in a relationship, he is my people.

And I had to get very clear on who my people *weren't* in order to recognize him.

It's not often that the heavens open up and drop your people on you in a small ski town. Whether it's on a dating app or out with friends, in the workplace or at a concert, you're not going to recognize them unless you know who you're looking for.

By the way, note that I didn't say you're looking for "the one." I'll paraphrase Dan Savage here when I tell you there's no such thing as "the one." You may find someone who is a .87. It's your choice whether you round them up to a one. And that's a daily choice on your part. I'll be diving into this further in "If It's Not a Fuck Yes, It's a No" in the next lesson.

But what I'm talking about now is looking at a solid .35 during your search and saying, "Hell, I can't be too picky."

Yes, you can! Be picky with your friends. Be picky with your lovers.

You've probably heard "You're the product of the five people you spend the most time with." Now, I don't think that's true. If your roommate blasts Bruce Springsteen all day (and if, like me, you're not a huge fan of the Boss), it doesn't mean you're going to be buying floor seats for his next tour. It *does* mean you'll have to put in your headphones, blast your music, and remind yourself of who you are.

If—because of circumstance or location, or just because you haven't found your people *yet*—you aren't surrounded by the messages you want to hear, create your own echo chamber. I did that by listening to nonstop *Savage Lovecast*. You might create yours through other podcasts or the social media accounts you follow.

The same is true for dating: don't fish in a lake if you're hoping to catch a shark. Don't turn to mainstream conventional dating apps when what you're craving is something outside the heterosexual-monogamous-vanilla box. Similarly, a hookup app isn't your best bet if you're looking to settle down and get married—it can happen, but that's not what the app is designed for. And striking out time and time again can leave you feeling like you're an island.

I worked with a client named Noemi who didn't feel like she belonged, in her social circle, on the apps. She's in her midforties, divorced a few years, and she spent most of her time with the same married friends she'd always socialized with. She felt like the third, fifth, seventh (you get the drift) wheel. And when she'd go out with her female friends one-on-one, they'd harangue her about needing to "get out there" and meet someone. These were her friends, but they weren't *her people*.

"I'm trying, but these dating apps are *awful*," Noemi complained. She was meeting boring men, having boring sex, and—just when she thought she'd found someone great—she's get ghosted..

It turned out the folks on these apps weren't her people either. What she was really craving was kinky sex, which she'd had once in her entire life but that had eluded her ever since.

"I don't even know if I want to settle down and live with someone again," she admitted, "but I do want to know what it's like to feel alive."

"Do your friends know this is what you're looking for?"

"Oh god no. They're as straitlaced as they come." Her friends had all followed the script. They'd landed good jobs and handsome husbands. Raised kids in their wealthy oceanfront community. "All they do is complain about their boring sex lives, though. It makes me a bit depressed being around them, to be honest. But the way they look down at me—the only divorced person in the group—makes me feel like a loser."

Instead of abandoning these relationships entirely, I suggested Noemi try out a different dating app that—I suspected—would yield her some better results.

Feeld.

Feeld is the app that I currently recommend most often: to clients, women I meet poolside in Palm Springs, hell, anyone who'll listen. Feeld is the place to go if you're looking for anything outside the hetero-mono-vanilla box. And despite being no stranger to dating apps, it blew Noemi's mind.

"The people on there are more mature and clear about what they want and don't want." She'd had a successful first date and another one lined up in the week since I'd last seen her. "I talked to him about my limits when it comes to pain, what I'm curious to try. I never would've thought I'd be able to talk so openly about these things."

And something else happened that week too. Noemi went out with her friends—the same ones she'd felt like an outsider with—and had a completely different experience. "I didn't even care that I was the only single person there. They even said to me, 'I've never seen you look this happy!'"

And that confidence persisted. During our final session, Noemi said, "I'm forty-four years old, and I feel like *me* for the first time in my life."

That, my friends, is the power of finding your people.

Maybe it's setting up a dating profile on Feeld. If you're curious about BDSM, search for a local "munch"—a social gathering of kinksters in a nonsexual setting like a coffee shop or restaurant—in your area. Most cities have sex-positive groups and meetups that *aren't* play parties (and if you're looking for play parties, I'll be chatting more about how to find them in "Make It a Group Thing" later in this book). If you're attracted to women but have limited experience hooking up with them, I'll give you some pointers in Lesson 15, "Go with the Flow."

If getting out there and meeting people in person seems like a giant leap, start with podcasts. It's beautiful that I can say there is no shortage whatsoever right now when it comes to sex-positive ones.

I promise you, there are people out there who share your core sexual values. Start looking for them!

If It's Not a Fuck
Yes, It's a No

was on the FlyAway Express bus from LAX to Union Station, my muffled tears fogging up the window beside me. My first husband sat to my left, completely oblivious.

We were on our way home from a four-day trip to a music festival in Chicago with friends, including a couple we knew well who'd become our travel buddies of sorts.

My husband had pulled his usual stunts: throwing tantrums and storming off while I somehow took the fall and issued apologies to our friends for his behavior. I was used to this cycle: placating to solve an argument or walking on eggshells to avoid one.

To give you some perspective, on the day of my law school graduation, I was late to meet up with some classmates I'd be carpooling with. Why? I went to the store to buy milk, because I feared one of the most important days of my life would devolve into a nuclear blowout if my husband woke up and was forced to drink his tea black.

This was *my* normal. But in Chicago, I realized this wasn't *normal.* We had another couple alongside us nearly every waking hour. I'd spent the last four days staring at a split screen: a healthy, functioning, and loving couple on one side...and us on the other.

On that bus ride home, I thought of those friends. And I thought of them again the next morning when I finally told my husband, "I can't do this anymore."

There's a widely accepted idea that "relationships are hard." This exact philosophy keeps folks in *bad* relationships all around the world every day. And I'm calling bullshit on it.

But there's an equally nefarious idea: that if things are *not* bad, then that's a good enough reason to stay. And for reasons you'll soon find out, I'll calling bullshit on that too.

A few years after my first husband and I split up, I got into a serious relationship with the kindest man I've ever dated. He was gentle and sweet and made me feel loved every day. I can count on one hand the number of arguments we had in two years.

Then we went ring shopping.

And then the dreams started.

Dreams of dates I'd had with guys a decade beforehand. Dreams of traveling on my own, of freedom. Every day for a month, I woke up with an emotional hangover, unsure what (if anything) my subconscious was shouting at me in my sleep. Until one day I woke up and whispered to myself, "Don't do this, Rena."

As I reflected on our relationship, I realized most of our fun revolved around our hobbies. Shopping for records together. Buying vintage clothes. And when I pictured the two of us growing old together—sipping lemonade side by side on a covered porch—I couldn't imagine what the hell we would talk about.

Unlike in my previous marriage, where I had an entire

library's worth of evidence as to why things were bad, I had nothing to point to in this relationship. Because it *wasn't* bad. Not in the slightest. This wasn't a hard relationship; this was an easy one.

But I wasn't a "fuck yes" about it.

I felt like the shittiest person on the face of the earth the day I broke up with him. He didn't deserve to be blindsided. He deserved all the happiness in the world. He deserved a love that would transcend time.

He deserved someone who was a fuck yes about him.

And that person wasn't me.

All my exes swore they'd never love again. And guess what? Every single one of them is now in a relationship with or married to someone who (appears to be) a waaay better match for them than I was or could ever be.

I talk to women on a nearly daily basis who choose to stay because they don't want to hurt their partner. Some of them are in unhealthy (maybe even borderline abusive) relationships (and if that's you, find the support you need to *get the fuck out*). But many are in lukewarm relationships, unable to point to anything that's "wrong," per se.

My client Makayla fell into the latter category. She'd never been the one to end a relationship.

"I normally wait until it dies on the other side, even if it's already dead with me." She came to me because she wanted to "grow a pair."

Makayla had been with her boyfriend for three years and had emotionally checked out. Before we started working together, she'd taken a consulting job that required her to live in different cities—apart from her partner—for months at a time. According to her, "When I go back to visit him, I feel like I'm in the past. When I'm here in this city, I'm in the future. I'm in limbo and want to find the present."

We began with a thought exercise: "Pretend you could wave a magic wand and end the relationship, knowing he would be fine with it. How would that make you feel?" I asked.

"I'd feel relieved. I'd feel...*free*."

And we dove deeper. She wanted to understand why she'd been in this pattern for so long and, in turn, make damned sure she wouldn't repeat it.

Her External Messaging Inventory revealed she'd carried on a tradition of being a martyr to her relationships.

"My parents taught me that you stay for the kids. You stay for the house. You stay for everything *but* your own happiness."

"And is that the message you want your relationship to embody?" I asked.

"Not at all. In a loving relationship, you're a really powerful being. They're a really powerful being. And together you make something big and beautiful. No one loses who they are."

Yet that wasn't the relationship she'd ended up in. By the time we started working together, she'd been on a "healing journey" for a year. She meditated daily. She read the books and listened to the podcasts (she'd discovered me through one, in fact). She was doing all the things that were *supposed* to bring her clarity. But she was more confused than ever.

And her health was suffering too. Every time she planned a trip back to see her boyfriend, her body would rebel, and she'd come down with a nasty cold.

"Listen, Makayla. I can tell you over and over again that you need to end this relationship. But I'm not your inner knowing."

Instead, we tapped into what her 80-year-old badass would say about the situation. During the exercise, she recalled a friendship she had in elementary school. "She was the cool kid and I never felt like I could speak up around her. I decided then that I needed to filter everything that comes out of my mouth. I need to formulate my words to make other people happy."

In other words, her job was to be liked, not to be honest. It was no surprise she'd ended up in a revolving door of mediocre relationships where she relied on her partners to sound the death knell.

Her 80-year-old badass cried out for a change: "You're settling for the bare fucking minimum right now, Makayla. This guy is only a blip in your entire life. Do whatever the fuck you want. There are a lot of other things you create that are so cool and make you so happy that none of these things fucking matter."

She listened to that inner knowing and ended things, finally walking out of the revolving mediocre-relationship door.

Sometimes, though, we wind up in relationships that aren't mediocre. Relationships that are better than the last one we had. "See, what an improvement!" we might think. And those relationships deserve even more scrutiny.

My client Shelby had been widowed for half a decade and finally began dating again. She met a man who lit her up in the bedroom, more than even her late husband had.

"The sex is great!" she told me. But when I probed further, she confessed he made no effort to help her orgasm. She also felt reluctant to bring up the idea of traveling together (despite yearning for a romantic getaway).

Another client, Kristen, was in a similar position: after being married for a decade to a man she wasn't sexually compatible with, she got serious with someone new.

Once again, "The sex is great!"

However, he claimed he wanted to indulge her kinky fantasies...but would then turn around and chastise her for "telling him what to do in the bedroom." He'd also disappear on booze benders for days at a time.

Both of these clients had been spellbound by "great" sex. But the sex itself wasn't *really* that great, was it? It was just better than what they'd experienced up until that point. A fresh 7-Eleven ham sandwich is better than a stale one, but it's still not a "great" sandwich. If you're starving—for sexual touch, for affection—you may end up eating whatever is put in front of you. But you *deserve* the highest quality.

Every relationship we have provides us an opportunity: to understand what we want *and* what we don't. Let me be clear: I'm not suggesting human beings are expendable or pawns in a larger game of self-discovery. My point is that we *all* deserve to be in a relationship where we feel a fuck yes about the other person and where our partner feels a fuck yes about us. There's nothing dignified about being with someone who's sticking around out of pity or obligation. Every day you stay with a person you're not a fuck yes about is a day you're holding them back from being with someone who's fuck yes about them; every day they stay with you is holding *you* back from the love you deserve.

Not all days will be fuck yes days. Some days, you'll argue.

Some days, the sound of your partner chewing will drive you to the brink of madness. It's what you do—how you live—most often that counts.

A day of fuck no doesn't turn the relationship into a no. A shitty day at work doesn't mean you quit your job tomorrow. One argument with a pal typically isn't the end of your friendship. Yet no one would fault you for leaving a job where you're being mistreated or switching careers so that you can find meaning in your life. People would understand if you ended a friendship with someone who you can't stand being around. We *need* money to survive. We *need* friends for our emotional well-being. We don't actually *need* romantic partners. Yet we've been brainwashed into accepting toxicity or ambivalence in our romantic relationships that we wouldn't stand for in other areas of our lives. Why? Because, as psychotherapist Esther Perel says, "In a world where it is so easy to feel insignificant—to be laid off, disposable, deleted with a click, unfriended—being *chosen* has taken on an importance it never has before." Our romantic relationships have become a holy grail.

An important fact about that holy grail: a relationship that ends isn't a failure. Author John Kim (a.k.a. The Angry Therapist) uses the term "expired relationships," which I find a more useful reframe.

"Like milk, your relationship has expired," he explains. "It had an expiration date. It was not meant to end one day sooner or one day later. Write this on your bathroom mirror. Read this out loud every day until you believe it." (And if you're looking to lick your wounds and find meaning after a breakup, I highly recommend John's book *Single. On Purpose.*)

I'm here to give you permission to fall out of love with what you thought you wanted. A hall pass to put yourself in the driver's seat of your life *and* your relationships. A reminder that ending things can be the kindest outcome on offer, not in the moment but in the long run. Sure, I've given (and will continue to give you) tips on how to love (and fuck) better. But in a world where women increasingly bear the emotional burden of "fixing" their relationships, my ultimate goal is to empower you to be in the type of relationship you want and deserve.

The kind boyfriend I told you about ended up marrying a friend of mine. I saw footage on social media from their wedding day—him crying at the altar, professing his undying love for her. My mean (to me) ex-husband eventually married a woman who brings out the best in him, and my heart swells when I see photos of them with their smiling child online. Our breakups made way for the types of relationships each of them thrives in. Relationships that—to me—appear like resounding fuck yeses.

Potential heartbreak is the price of admission we pay to be in a relationship, but enduring pain to *stay* in a relationship is a choice. That choice can come from fear ("I'll never find someone who loves me like they do!"), obligation ("I don't want our kids to go through a divorce!"), logistical concerns ("It's easier to stay together than move out and find a new place!"), or shame ("I'm a bad person if I hurt them!").

There is no one-size-fits-all definition for a "healthy" relationship. My partner and I live apart and don't spend every night together. Some people might label that as some sort of noncommittal red flag when in fact this is the healthiest relationship I've ever been in. So no. I'm not going to give you a long checklist to gauge whether your relationship is healthy or not. Instead, I'm going to pose some questions, below, which I'll invite you to stop, seriously consider, and record your answers to:

- Are you excited to spend time with this person?
- Are they your cheerleader when it comes to big life goals?
- Do you feel physically and emotionally safe around them?
- Do you feel like you can have hard conversations?
- Are they putting equal effort into the relationship?
- Are you physically attracted to them?
- Do they make *you* feel physically attractive?
- Do you feel better (as opposed to worse) about yourself as a result of being in a relationship with them?

If the answer to all of the above is yes, then great! You probably have a functioning and healthy relationship. But as I mentioned earlier, healthy and functioning doesn't automatically mean a fuck yes.

So dive a bit deeper and record your answers to these questions:

- What is the purpose of a relationship?
- What does a healthy relationship look like?
- What is romantic love?

Does your current relationship look like the one you just described? If the answer is no, ask yourself: is there a realistic chance we can get there?

Note that I said "realistic." If you two can't have a discussion without it turning into an argument and, for example, your partner says they'll never in a million years go to couples therapy, then it's probably not realistic to think your relationship will change. If your idea of romantic love is raising a family together and your partner keeps talking about getting a vasectomy, you're definitely not on the same page.

On the other hand, if you want to be more physically active together and your partner has started going on walks with you, give it a reasonable amount of time and space to see if there's a way to meet your needs. If there's *sustained* effort being shown, then offer your partner the benefit of the doubt.

If you've determined there's no realistic chance your relationship will become what you'd like it to be, *why are you staying?*

Is it because of fear? Obligation? Logistics? Shame?

Now imagine we could wave the magic wand and erase whatever it is that's keeping you there. The kids would be perfectly fine. You could teleport into a new living situation. Both of you would be emotionally sound after the breakup.

Now, how do you feel?

Do you feel relief and freedom, like Makayla did?

Do you feel some sadness but ultimately hope about the future?

Or do you feel like part of your heart would be ripped out of your chest? (Hint: this is a fuck yes.)

Most importantly, what would your 80-year-old badass say? Get into the head of the 80-year-old, most sage, wise, badass version of you. What would she tell you to do about this relationship? Would she tell you to stay or go?

Love isn't a cost-benefit analysis. There's no formula or

algorithm when it comes to matters of the heart. But your inner knowing—your 80-year-old badass—she knows what a fuck yes is. In the next lesson, I'll talk about being fuck yes about someone in terms of sexual compatibility.

12

Do It Soon

The sex education you received probably espoused abstinence (and made no mention whatsoever of pleasure). Your religion may have beat into your mind that sex—between a man and a woman only, of course—"should" be saved until marriage. Your mom may have told you to "make him wait." Your friends might joke about not "giving it up" too quickly. Or maybe you have a "no sex until the third date" rule.

When it comes down to the timing of sex, everyone has an opinion. And what all these opinions have in common is the idea that we, as women, have something that we're using as a bargaining chip in the relationship. These nuggets of advice reinforce the idea that sex isn't ours; we're merely its gatekeepers.

I was never one to wait to have sex, and when I did, it was usually because of circumstances outside my control (e.g., being on my period) when I met the person. I had my fair share of one-night stands. If I saw relationship potential with someone, I'd normally suss them out on the first date, then sleep with them the second.

Except one time.

We'd started seeing each other, and he was nice as hell. He planned cute outings to art galleries and made mimosas in the morning. I introduced him to my friends really quickly. We saw each other most days, and within weeks, it was apparent we were heading into boyfriend/girlfriend territory.

But I'd waited. And not just to have intercourse with him; I'd waited to do anything remotely sexual with him. We would kiss. We would fall asleep next to each other in pajamas, cuddling through the night. I felt safe with him. I liked him.

"We haven't done it yet," I proudly declared to my girlfriends. This was Rena, reformed. This was Rena, doing the thing most women did: holding on to her chastity like some prize that needed to be won.

A month in, I gave up the prize. And I learned my lesson.

The sex was fine. It wasn't bad by any means. But it wasn't a fuck yes either. If we'd done it earlier, there's a good chance our relationship would've fizzled out relatively quickly. But by this point, I was in over my head: to him, to my friends. Everything else on paper was so damned good. I couldn't break up with him just because the sex was "fine"...could I? What kind of asshole would that make me?

Instead we remained on the relationship escalator. The boyfriend and girlfriend labels were affixed. Families were met. Weddings were attended. A housewarming party was thrown. He was an attentive lover—not selfish by any means—but we didn't have that sexual fire burning between us. No hungrily kissing and ripping each other's clothes off. I would come. He would come. Then we'd fall asleep cuddling.

In hindsight, that month I'd waited to sleep with him had told me everything I'd needed to know. Why? *Because it had been easy to wait.* And it was easy precisely *because* we didn't have that fire burning between us.

When we eventually broke up, I moved in with a friend temporarily until I found a landing spot. My first night at the house, I got into a conversation with her male roommate in the kitchen.

"I heard you two broke up. What happened?" he asked. He'd known my boyfriend casually through the occasional party we'd attended together.

"I don't actually have a good reason as to why," I told him. "We had a ton of fun together. We liked to go on adventures."

He then declared, with no hesitation whatsoever, "That's all friend stuff, Rena."

I'll never forget those words.

Because yes. We were friends. We were the best of friends. We were two people who were probably never meant to be in a romantic relationship at all.

Now, if you and your partner both want to be in a companionate relationship—where you two don't have sex—that's perfectly fine. This might be especially appealing to people on the asexual spectrum—who do not experience sexual attraction to others. For us allosexual (i.e., *not* asexual) folks, though, sex is the thing that separates friends from lovers. Sex is what separates family from lovers, coworkers from lovers. Sex—above all else—is what makes a romantic relationship just that. Yet it's the one thing we're told to wait to do. It's the single area of compatibility that defines a relationship and often the last one we examine.

In his book *Savage Love from A to Z*, Dan Savage points out:

It's always amazed me that so many people refuse to prioritize sexual compatibility like they do everything else… In the early stages of a relationship, people obsess over the number of children they'd like to have…dogs or cats, *90 Day Fiancé* or *Selling Sunset*. But they can't pause for a moment to ask themselves if this otherwise lovely person they're dating fucks them the way they like to be fucked, and fucks them as often as they'd like to be fucked, because that would make them shallow, sex-obsessed perverts.

The messages we get about sex are maddeningly contradictory. Sex is at once utterly trivial, certainly not something a good person attaches too much importance to, and at the same time it's so important, so sacred to the partner bond, that you aren't allowed to do it with anyone else.

I'm challenging you to ignore those messages from the very inception stage of the relationship. The getting-to-know-you-to-see-if-I-want-to-keep-getting-to-know-you stage. Because if you wait too long to get to know the person sexually, you're missing out on valuable data on whether you two are suited for each other. Knowing what each of your expectations, wants, needs, and desires are at the starting line can make (or break) the relationship as it twists and turns.

Does this mean you need to hop into bed with someone the first night you meet them? No, that's not what I'm saying. I'm also not saying you need to jump straight into oral sex or intercourse. I'm simply calling bullshit on the "wait as long as you can" idea of sex and replacing it with "have it as soon as you want to."

Say you *don't want* to get sexual right away. Not because you've been brainwashed into thinking you need to make a person wait but because you need an emotional connection first in order to become sexually attracted to someone. I'd still encourage you to get curious and find other ways to determine sexual compatibility early. I mean in the same way you'd get curious about, for instance, what kind of food they like. If you're a total foodie and they turn their nose at anything you can't get at McDonald's, it's probably not a good match. But say they're not well versed in food but are *open and curious* to try new things? Ding! This isn't about finding someone who orders the same sushi roll off the menu; this is determining that you share core values when it comes to pleasure. (And if you need a refresher on what those values are, take a look back at the 27 Things exercise you completed in Lesson 1!)

Bringing it back to the idea of sex: have a heavy make-out session if you're up for it. Open a conversation about whether they have any kinks and what sex means to them. Find out what their views are on toys in the bedroom. Are they big on foreplay? What's their stance on monogamy?

If you prefer to take things slowly to build up desire and anticipation, which is absolutely fair (and can be super hot!), lean in to the idea of first base, second base, etc. Gather as much data as you possibly can: Is this person a good kisser? Does it seem like they prioritize my needs too? Am I excited to keep exploring with them? You don't have to have every item on the

menu before deciding you like the restaurant, but if the appe-
tizers are shit, it'll tell you a lot about what to expect from the
main course.

Regardless of how long you choose to wait, please remember:
every day you spend waiting to see if you're sexually compatible
with someone could be a day wasted. Every day you invest in
someone outside the bedroom will make it harder to end things
if what happens in the bedroom isn't up to par.

Ever heard of the term *decoy baby*? I hadn't until a friend of
mine had kids. Her first son didn't cry through the night. He was
a loving and well-mannered toddler. *Wow! Being a mom is easy!*
she thought to herself. Her second child was none of the above.
He was colicky and temperamental as a baby and grew into a very
headstrong boy (much like his mama, we joke).

"I realize my first son was a decoy baby," she'd tell us. "He
tricked me into expecting motherhood would always be easy."

Decoy lovers are out there. They talk a big game and turn out
to be either completely selfish in the bedroom or not nearly as
skilled as they claim to be (or sometimes both).

My client Cecilia met one when she opened up her sexless
marriage. They'd started talking on a dating app and quickly
moved their conversion to Snapchat. Photos were exchanged.
She was honest with him about only wanting a sexual relationship outside her marriage. He was okay with this being her first
time with another man and agreed to take things slowly.

They met up for coffee, which turned into a make-out session
in his car. After feeling dead below the waist for years, Cecilia
was reborn. "I felt like flowers were coming out of my head!"
she said during our next session. They continued their Snapchat

conversation and made a plan to take it further the next time they met. She bought lingerie in anticipation.

"This is the start of a new me," she said excitedly.

And then they had sex.

"It wasn't good. He was like a jackrabbit."

Womp-womp.

She'd even tried to guide him, showing him what turned her on, to no avail. These were two people who'd spent weeks building up chemistry and who—in the end—weren't sexually compatible with each other. He'd been a decoy lover. He'd spent all his effort on creating the perfect appetizer and none on the main course.

A few weeks was a blip on the radar of her life. This man had woken her up...then led her into a cold shower. She'd learned a lesson, but at least she'd learned it quickly.

People say you learn a lot about a person by how they treat a waiter. I say the only way to truly know if someone is good in bed is to sleep with them.

"So if the first time is bad, does that mean I should call it quits right away?"

Not necessarily. And here's why.

The first time can be awkward, for a host of reasons. Feeling nervous. Seeing them naked. Exposing *yourself* for the first time. Maybe they use a word in the bedroom ("cock," "pussy," or "daddy," for example) that throws you right out of the mood. And maybe if they knew this, they wouldn't have done it in the first place. Give lovers the benefit of the doubt...to an extent.

I hate to use the term *red flags* because it's so unambiguous. At the same time, if you're reading this book, you're looking for guidance, and I want to be as specific as I possibly can be. So let's call these bright pink flags (BPFs). If you see one of these your first time in the bedroom with someone, there had better be a damned good reason to give them a second shot.

They Don't Prioritize Your Pleasure

Note, I'm not saying they don't give you an orgasm. For some women (I'm one of them!), the stars have to align just right to climax on the first go-round...and those stars align as infrequently as a solar eclipse. But if they don't care about it at all? That's a BPF. It's the difference between politely declining the chips and salsa at a restaurant versus not being offered them in the first place.

They Act without Consent

A guy once slapped me across the face the first time we had sex. I'm not into being slapped across the face the fiftieth time I have sex with someone, much less the first. He would know that if he'd asked. If someone doesn't ask your consent before hurting you, it's a huge BPF.

But we don't need to be talking about pain in order for consent to be relevant. Consent applies to *everything*. Are they weird about using protection? Are they sticking something into your ass without asking first? Are they secretly taking photos or videos? Huge BPFs.

They Shame You

Shaming can manifest in myriad ways in the bedroom.

"Why do you need *that*?" when you pull out a vibrator.

"Why haven't you come yet?" can be another one.

If you're feeling like there's something wrong or deficient with you because of the way your body looks, how it works, or what you're into, it's a BPF.

These are the biggies. Anything that didn't make it onto this list comes down to personal preference. Your BPF might be that there wasn't oral before intercourse or that they showed you their entire bondage collection when you expressed no interest whatsoever in kink. In the spirit of not yucking anyone's yum, I'd urge you to err on the side of fewer BPFs rather than more while also honoring your core sexual values. Either way, it's best to know what you're signing up for as soon as you can.

13

Stop Playing the Cool Girl

Men always say that as the defining compliment, don't they? She's a cool girl… Cool Girls never get angry; they only smile in a chagrined, loving manner and let their men do whatever they want. Go ahead, shit on me, I don't mind, I'm the Cool Girl… They're not even pretending to be the woman they want to be, they're pretending to be the woman a man wants them to be… [H]e wants Cool Girl, who is basically the girl who likes every fucking thing he likes and doesn't ever complain. (How do you know you're not Cool Girl? Because he says things like: "I like strong women." If he says that to you, he will at some point fuck someone else. Because "I like strong women" is code for "I hate strong women.")

Gone Girl, Gillian Flynn

By the time I met my first husband, I had mastered playing the Cool Girl. It started as a way to shield myself from heartbreak—which I knew all too well by that point—but soon became a game all its own.

I'd become adept at getting most men to fall for me. Coy remarks. A nervous "Aw, I love you too" once they said the words for the first time. I played the game to win: win the guy, win the engagement ring, win the happily ever after that we're supposed to want.

We met on a dance floor in Brighton, my junior year of college, but I'd noticed him the second he'd walked in the club door. I turned to my study-abroad classmate and whispered, "*That's my type.*"

He was tall, with a mop of brown hair on his head and intense blue eyes. Fashionably dressed. Incredibly handsome. Way, way too handsome for me actually. But I was a stranger in a strange land and decided to shoot my shot anyway. I had no idea at that point that he was accustomed to dating models (but it didn't surprise me when I eventually found out).

I kept my distance and waited for my opening. When we eventually danced alongside one another to some '60s song being spun on vinyl, I made my move.

"Nice tie," I told him as I slid his piece of vintage macramé between my fingers.

He looked down. "It *is* a nice tie. But it's a bit frayed at the bottom."

"Oh, I could fix that," I said, already turning my back to him and dancing with no one.

He'd later recount the story to friends and family as some sort of romantic gesture. How he knew I was "special."

"She offered to fix my tie for me!" he'd tell them, thinking I was already interested in helping and supporting him. Really, I was coming from a place of knowing it all. Not fawning over him, knowing better than him. I was being a cocky little shit.

We became inseparable. He traveled home with me for Thanksgiving. And then for Christmas, where my mother pulled me aside and whispered, "If he asks you to marry him, you say yes."

He'd fallen in love with a version of me who had very few responsibilities. Yes, I was a student at the time. A student without a car or a job. A young woman who found it fun to play house, to have elaborate meals cooked from scratch waiting for him when he walked through the door after work. A nineteen-year-old who doted on a man ten years her senior and held him on a pedestal like some sort of Adonis.

He hadn't fallen in love with a strong woman.

"Things are going to change when we move to the United States," I said. "My course load will be more demanding. I'll be studying for the LSAT and applying to law school."

In other words, I wouldn't have the luxury of playing the Cool Girl anymore, the girl he *had* fallen in love with. I'd be putting my big girl pants on and getting down to work.

Everything changed. Of course it did. Once I started using my voice, he began raising his. I couldn't keep up the facade anymore, pretending I had no needs. The next five years were a tug-of-war that never would've happened had I not been wearing a mask in the first place.

To say our marriage ended badly is a massive understatement. But I hadn't learned my lesson yet. Because above all, I'd found a winning formula. A successful, brilliant, shockingly good-looking Englishman had moved across an ocean to commit his life to me. The proof was in the (sticky toffee) pudding.

Once our marriage ended, I doubled down. I read *Men Are from Mars, Women Are from Venus* in one sitting. My copy of *Why Men Love Bitches* was graffitied with highlights, notes, and Post-it flags.

I became the friend whose friends asked what to text back. I was the one who encouraged them to curb their enthusiasm. To remain aloof. To say, "Yeah, sounds great" when their courter would suggest plans.

I played the same game. I got the same results. Results that were exactly what I wanted at first but that turned into a prison of my own making. I was great at getting onto the relationship escalator, but I never liked the view from the top.

Several long-term relationships and another marriage later, I decided to call it quits.

"Listen, I know the game. I've been playing it my whole life. And I don't want to do it anymore," I said to my (now) partner, candle-light flickering as we sat across from each other on our first date.

This one statement flew in the face of every piece of dating advice I'd read. Telling someone you're not going to play the game implies you've been played.

"I won't play games with you either," he told me. "If I don't text back right away, it's because I work with my phone in the other room. It's not because I'm 'making you wait.'"

And I knew right then he'd played the game before too.

We were both waving our respective white flags. Promising each other we'd do better this time around.

We bought each other Christmas ornaments on our next date. A few months in, he tied a bundle of lilies to the front gate of my house ("from a secret admirer," the note read) while—unbeknownst to him—I was secretly hiding a gift near his front door, like a sappy, lovesick ninja.

And when he eventually told me he loved me, I responded in a way I never had before.

I sobbed.

"I love you too," I blubbered.

"Then why are you crying?" he asked.

"Because I'm scared you're going to break my fucking heart."

"Why would you say that?"

"Because it's what I deserve."

And I fully believed that. This was my cosmic karma. I was destined to know what it was like to have my heart smashed into pieces as I'd done with my own sledgehammer in most of my adult relationships.

"We've both hurt people. But we were different people then," he explained, holding my hand. "And we've done the work on ourselves. You deserve to be happy. *We* deserve to be happy."

I felt a million things in that moment but most of all vulnerable. As Brené Brown says, "Staying vulnerable is a risk we have to take if we want to experience connection."

As I now say, "You can be the Cool Girl, or you can have true love. *Pick one.*"

"Wait, Rena. How do I know if I'm playing the Cool Girl?" you might wonder.

Here's one way to find out.

Open up your text messages.

Compare the messages you've sent to romantic interests and the ones you've sent to friends.

Are they *noticeably* different from each other?

Are you waiting to respond?

Are you holding back the same excitement you normally express when you're making plans with a close friend?

Do the messages look like they've been written by two different versions of you?

If the answer to any of these questions is yes, there's a good chance you're playing the Cool Girl, even if you aren't doing it deliberately.

You may be thinking to yourself, "This is bullshit. If I want to be treated like a prize, I need to make them chase me."

Sure, that's one way of doing it. And look where it got me.

Instead, *show* them you're a prize. Show them the side of you that's enthusiastic. That's willing to get hurt. People fall in love with real people, not life-size cardboard cutouts.

Does this exponentially increase your chances of getting hurt? Abso-fucking-lutely. But the reward on the other end is so worth it. You'll miss out on seeing the world if you're too scared to hop on a plane. All the best things in life come with risk. Love is no different.

I worked with a client, Casey, who'd been the Cool Girl. Aloof. Emotionally unavailable. Men fell for her all the time. Mainly artists, desperately looking to unlock her inner world through the lenses of their cameras or strokes of their brushes.

She played the part well but wanted the charade to end.

"I want to be able to ask people out instead of waiting for them to ask me out. I want to feel safe not wearing makeup. I want to feel like I can share my insecurities with my partner the way I do with my girlfriends."

Her attraction—inside and out—had been carefully curated. Newly single (after breaking yet another artist's heart), she wanted to date differently. She wanted to date *as herself*. And that was a foreign concept to her. Even as a young child, she played a role. Her father—an alcoholic—brought her to bars with him when she was as young as six years old. She had to be seen and not heard. She wasn't allowed to say, "Hey, Dad. I'd rather be at the playground than watching you get drunk."

My client Alison was also the dutiful daughter. As a child, she was rewarded for excelling in school. Love was something you got through performing; affection wasn't handed out for its own sake. As a result, she'd become "a cold bitch" as an adult. By the time we started working together, she was divorced and in a relationship with a caring, gentle man who was helping her raise her children.

"I don't know how to show him affection. I don't even know how to show my kids affection." She was the bad cop to his good. And she began to worry that she'd pass down to her kids the same coldness she'd experienced as a child. "I want to do better."

Casey and Alison each wore masks: Casey in the form of makeup and a perfect appearance, Alison in the form of her ice-cold armor. Both of them were Cool Girls, although they expressed it differently.

But the solution for both of them was the same: express your emotions.

With Casey, that began with canceling plans that she'd agreed to but was never really interested in in the first place. She started being proactive on dating sites, sending the first message to men she was interested in, politely declining the rest.

Alison started sending voice memos and texts to her partner throughout the day. And not just "Hey, can you pick up some milk on the way home?" type of texts. I suggested she text *him* exactly the sorts of things she'd told me *about him* during our sessions. She told him she loved him. She thanked him for being a good man.

These small gestures created seismic changes in both their lives. Casey eventually met a man and decided to take the relationship slow to make sure she wasn't settling, once again. She became the artist of her own life and openly told him what she was into sexually and started planning dates for the two of them without fear of being unpalatable or too controlling.

Alison went from being the "cool girl" to the "cool mom," planning game nights and ice cream sundae fests for her kids for no reason at all—bringing in the warmth she'd missed. She even opened up to her partner about her BDSM fantasies.

"This isn't just a new chapter in my life," she told me during our final session. "It's a new *book*."

So how do you avoid falling into Cool Girl mode? How do you stop contorting yourself to fit someone else's ideal or pretending like you have no needs at all?

Start by getting clear on what you want.

Earlier, you compiled your list of 27 Things. Look at that list of desires again. Whether you're in a relationship or wanting to be in one, ask yourself: am I compromising my needs? And then, get more granular.

Spend some time writing about what your ideal day with a partner would look like. Imagine it from the moment you wake up to the moment you fall asleep at night. Pick a weekend/non-work day.

Here are some snapshots from former Shameless clients:

Wake up around 10:00 a.m. and cook breakfast for us, probably an omelet or French toast (my favorites).

Watch *Law & Order* or any show for a few hours.

Talk about what we want out of our lives. Our careers. Where we want to move. When should we give up on having a baby if we haven't gotten pregnant. Our progress.

By 1:00 or 2:00 p.m., we go out to do a fun activity like sip and paint or movies and listen to our audiobook on the way.

Go to dinner around 6:00 p.m.

Come home, shower, and relax and cuddle.

Watch a show on TV.

By 8:00 or 9:00 p.m., light a candle and have sex.

———————

We start by waking up after spending the night together. We each possibly have our own places but alternate spending nights with each other depending on what's happening. We start the day with some early morning sex and time to lounge and cuddle, which could take up to a few hours. We then go to Sunday brunch and then hit up the farmers' market. By now, we've made it to early afternoon and decide to take a bike ride or visit a museum. After a couple of hours, we get home and make an early Sunday dinner. Later in the evening, we cuddle up and watch a movie to wind down from our day together.

———————

8:00 a.m.–9:00 a.m.: Wake up, have morning sex.

9:00 a.m.–12:00 p.m.: Get ready for the day and grab brunch.

12:00 p.m.–2:00 p.m.: Relax, nap.

2:00 p.m.–4:00 p.m.: Do a physical activity like hike, walk, bike, spend time with our dog.

4:00 p.m.–6:00 p.m.: Get ready separately for a dinner.

6:30 p.m.–8:30 p.m.: Dinner out to someplace new.

8:30 p.m.–10:30 p.m.: Drinks at a fun bar or go to a show.

10:30 p.m.: Head home, more drinks, and sex.

He makes me coffee in the morning and then gives me quiet space to write in my journal, meditate, and feel grounded with myself.

We do something active, like a hike or a walk on the beach, and then get lunch/brunch sitting outside somewhere with a beautiful view.

(I am having a hard time imagining wanting to spend an entire day with someone. It is interesting. I think the pandemic made me feel like I need more time to myself to recharge. Like, what I described above sounds great, but then I feel like I need him to give me time alone for the afternoon afterward.)

Dinner together, ideally with other friends too, perhaps play games—anything that is playful and laughter-filled. Snuggle up on the couch afterward, feeling at ease (at home) with him and also both comforted and excited by his touch.

There's a difference between compromising with someone and abandoning yourself. If you're in a relationship, ask your partner to complete their own version of the exercise. Then sit down and compare yours. Is the relationship lopsided when it comes to whose needs take priority? Are you bending more than they are? If the answer is yes to both of those questions, it's time to speak up.

Say you're single and starting to date. You're welcome to ask any prospects what *their* version of an ideal day is (this is also generally a great way to connect and get to know people). If you find out someone's idea of a perfect date night is getting wasted at the club till 2:00 a.m. and you'd prefer to Netflix and chill? You'll probably wind up spending a lot of your evenings apart from each other and not, well, "dating." (I've been on both sides of that one.) Or if someone envisions living separately from a partner and you're looking to move in at some point? Again, one of you will have to bend on a nontrivial lifestyle choice. And—Cool Girl beware—it'll probably be you.

Am I saying that if you don't find someone who has the exact same view of an ideal day that they're not right for you? Not at all. My partner's day begins with waking up at 5:00 a.m. and immediately making a huge breakfast. I'd prefer to sleep in and have morning sex and wait until lunch to eat. I know this about him. He knows this about me. I don't pretend to like breakfast, and he lets me sleep in. The key here is to figure out whether you're going to feel *resentful* because of those incompatibilities or compromises.

The Cool Girl facade can only last so long. Stop acting and start living!

Examine Your Default Setting

Y ou may be wondering why a women's intimacy coach is leading this group," I began, looking out at the group of gay men attending an ethical nonmonogamy master class. "Clearly, you're not my target client base. But I know what it's like to be closeted."

What these men all have in common is a shared shame, one rooted in their Christian faith. A belief system that told them if they just tried "hard enough," they could conform. This was a group of men who'd tried to do just that—many of whom had been married to women, wondering why they couldn't get this damned thing right—and failed miserably.

I knew that pain. I lived that shame.

I talk about ethical nonmonogamy (ENM) *a lot*. On social media. In master classes (such as the one I just mentioned). In workshops for hundreds of women at a time.

And it's the most polarizing topic I speak about. More so than kink or BDSM. More so than female sexual fluidity or sexual fantasies.

I had a friend tell me recently she'd had to mute me on Instagram. "Your content about nonmonogamy was really triggering for me. Is there something wrong with me that I just want to be with one person?"

So let's start there.

I'm not here to "sell you" on ENM.

Seriously, I'm not.

Because I contorted myself to try to fit the mold that society told me was the "right" way of being, the last thing I want is to shame you into thinking there's something wrong with you for wanting what you want.

I'm asking you to examine your default setting. Keep that in mind as you keep reading. And I do urge you to keep reading. Even if you're convinced this chapter doesn't apply to you, there'll be lessons here that you can take into your current or future relationships. Or at the very least, you'll be a better ally to people around you who choose to live and love differently.

Even if you think you don't know anyone who is practicing ENM, there's a hell of a good chance you know (or will know) people who practice *unethical* nonmonogamy, i.e., cheating. When it comes to infidelity rates, it's hard to pin down an exact number, because people don't like to admit they've committed infidelity, and what constitutes "cheating" varies widely. Is watching porn cheating? How about signing up for a dating app but never meeting anyone in person? Does an emotional affair count? Do we draw the line at kissing? Intercourse?

In her book *Untrue*, Wednesday Martin points out that "statistics range from as low as 13 percent to as high as 50 percent of women admitting they have been unfaithful to a spouse or partner; many experts suggest the numbers might well be higher."

Even if we can't get our finger on a precise number, Martin tells us there's a general consensus that the infidelity gap between men and women is closing. In other words, year by year, women are cheating more, and men's infidelity rates have stayed pretty constant.

Martin goes on to highlight the fact that "95 percent of respondents in a nationally representative sample of cohabitating and married American adults expected monogamy of their partners and believed their partners expected it of them."

In other words: almost all of us expect monogamy, but we're really shitty at it.

And there's shame that comes with straying. The shame of being cheated on *and* the shame of being the one who cheats. Infidelity creates a shame cesspool. It's time to have an honest dialogue about what it would mean to bring this shame out of the shadows and how we can ethically practice what we've been doing unethically for so long.

But there's more to this story too.

Back in Lesson 10, "Find Your People," I mentioned a woman who was in the poly processing group with me and who couldn't get over her jealousy when her partner was out on dates with others. I've seen similar frustrations with some of my clients. Just as there's a shame that comes along with cheating when the default setting is monogamy, some women are feeling defective for not being "good" at ENM.

Miranda, for example was in hierarchical poly relationships for most of her adult life and lived in a major metropolitan city where ENM felt like the norm in her age demographic. She and her partner had been together for nearly a decade but had had other boyfriends and girlfriends outside the relationship.

"We both went to Burning Man one year, except he stayed at a different camp with his *other* girlfriend," she said. "I barely saw him and spent most of the festival crying."

This type of emotional anguish had become the norm for her. She kept thinking if she tried harder—read more books, continued therapy for her "anxious attachment style"—that she'd arrive at some level of enlightenment that would shield her from feelings of jealousy and insecurity.

I worked with another woman, Alexis, who enjoyed going to play parties—sometimes alone, sometimes with whoever her partner happened to be at the time—and would swing with other couples. It was her community, a safe place where she'd forged close friendships. "It's fun, but I sometimes fantasize about just being in a committed relationship. One man, one woman. Is there something wrong with me?"

Succumbing to social pressures, both clients had clung to a default setting that *wasn't* monogamy. Yet the shame persisted.

Whether your default setting is ENM or monogamy, examine it. Challenge it.

Ask yourself, "Is this actually what I want?"

And while you ask that, be open about your options, especially ones you're rejecting on principle.

"God, these dating apps are a fucking nightmare. *Everyone* is poly now," a friend lamented to me over cocktails. It wasn't the first time I'd heard a similar complaint, and as ENM becomes less taboo and increasingly more mainstream, I'm positive it won't be the last.

"Well, what is it you're looking for?"

"I just want regular monogamy!"

"Okay, be more specific. Imagine you could wave the magic wand: what would your ideal relationship look like?"

"I want to find my person. Maybe a few years in, once we're stable and in love and secure, we can look into having a threesome. And, you know, if he's out of town or I'm out of town and there's a onetime hookup that happens, it's not the end of the world. Just be safe and don't exchange numbers and don't bring the relationship home with you."

She'd fallen into a trap I see often: assuming that monogamy and polyamory are the only two, mutually exclusive options rather than poly being just one of many types of ENM. Saying you want monogamy because you're not into poly arrangements is like saying you don't like fruit because you're not into bananas. Just because poly doesn't appeal to you doesn't mean you need to throw the proverbial ENM baby out with the bathwater.

Think of ENM as a large umbrella, with lots of relationship practices and styles underneath it. If you're looking to dive deeper into the world of ENM, here are some books to get you started:

- *Polysecure* by Jessica Fern
- *Opening Up* by Tristan Taormino
- *Designer Relationships* by Mark A. Michaels and Patricia Johnson

In the meantime, I'll provide you with a (nonexhaustive) list of ENM styles, including a few examples.

- **Polyamory:** Many loves. You have multiple concurring relationships (e.g., a husband *and* a girlfriend). Typically all partners know about each other.
- **Swinging:** You (and a partner, if you have one) hook up with other couples or singles. These interactions tend to be primarily sexual and wouldn't rise to the level of being in a relationship with the other parties.
- **Monogamish:** A term coined by Dan Savage. For all intents and purposes, you're in a monogamous relationship, but if a one-time thing happens, it's not the end of the world (or relationship). It's up to you whether you want to disclose or know about the indiscretion or implement a don't ask, don't tell (DADT) policy.

What my friend had described was a blend of DADT, monogamish (one-time hookups outside the relationship that she didn't want to know about), and swinging (having threesomes with a partner). In other words, *not monogamy.*

Take some time to think about this for yourself. If you could design your own type of relationship, what would it look like? And if that feels too overwhelming (we don't know what we don't know, after all), use these five Ws as a jumping-off point. Be sure to write down your answers!

WHO?

- Who would be involved? Meaning, are we playing together, separately, or both?
- Is anyone (friends, mutual acquaintances, coworkers, etc.) off-limits?

WHAT?

- What is allowed? Dates? One-night stands?
- Do we draw the line at kissing? Oral? Penetration?

WHERE?

- If we share a bed, is that off-limits for us to play alone in?
- Is this only okay at a play party or some other "neutral" zone?
- If one of us is traveling for work, would a hookup be okay? Does it need to be in another zip code...state...country?

WHEN?

- Can this happen when we're out together, or is this only when we're apart?
- Do we need to talk about this beforehand?
- Do we want a DADT policy?

WHY?

- Why do I want to do this?
- Why is it important for me to do this?

I want to elaborate on the why a bit more, as it's nuanced. For some folks (myself included), being ENM is a fundamental part of our sexual identity. I felt stifled in relationships where monogamy was the default setting. I've also had bisexual clients express they couldn't be in a primary relationship where they wouldn't be allowed to have sex with people of a different gender because they would stifle the full range of their sexual expression.

And there are people who aren't hardwired for it but choose ENM for practical reasons, like the following:

- You're into BDSM but your partner isn't. You have an agreement that you can play with other partners to have your kinky needs met.
- You've been together for a long time and want to branch out and bring some novelty into your relationship in the form of a threesome (or moresome!).
- You're in a long-distance relationship and want to have your sexual and affectionate needs met with someone closer to home.

Everyone's why is unique to them. If ENM appeals to you, write down why. And as a follow-up, question whether practicing ENM is necessary for you to express the full range of your sexuality.

Understand it may take some time to determine your why. My client Chloe and I began working together as she was trying to repair her marriage. "I confessed to him I'd been essentially cheating on him since day one," which was about fifteen years ago, she told me. She figured if perhaps they could be more aligned sexually, more attuned emotionally, then it would solve her wandering eye. Or at the very least, she wanted to see if it would.

In the end, Chloe and her husband kept their relationship closed but still started having *great* sex. They indulged in BDSM and role-play. He made her squirt for the first time. They leaned into hard conversations instead of avoiding them. For all intents and purposes, her marriage now looked exactly as she wanted it to.

"But I still want to cheat on him," she confessed during our last session. And she didn't deem herself a failure for it. "I thought fixing the marriage would solve my desire to be with other people, but it hasn't."

And that itself was clarity.

Chloe thought she wanted ENM for pragmatic reasons: I'm not having my needs met, so I'll meet them elsewhere. Once her husband was able to meet those needs, she understood she's actually wired for ENM, which wasn't an option in that marriage. Her why changed.

So once you have a clear(ish) understanding about what you'd like to explore, how do you start talking about it?

Whether you're planted firmly in the monogamy camp or ENM camp (or somewhere in between), be honest. Say you're single and using online dating platforms. Your bio could include phrases like these:

- Only interested in monogamy.
- Curious to explore ENM.
- Pansexual and want to play with different genders.

Yes, *be that direct.* Will it send some people swiping left? Sure it will. But it'll also invite in your people. Don't be the ENM version of the douchebag who pretends he's looking for love then fucks you and ghosts. *Be up front.*

But let's say you're in a relationship that's been built with monogamy as its default setting, and you realize later you want to flip the switch. That can feel fucking terrifying. The conversation itself can shatter a foundation of trust between two people and leave your partner feeling insecure and rejected. On the other hand, sucking it up and praying and hoping things will change will only breed resentment on your end (trust me, I know).

So how do you honor your own wants, needs, and desires while also broaching the subject compassionately?

Baby. Steps.

Start off with asking your partner how they feel about monogamy generally. And give it some context. Whenever I'm teaching a workshop and women ask, "Okay, so how do I bring this up to my partner?" I tell them to throw me under the bus.

"Oh, I was in a workshop today, and the instructor brought up XYZ. What do you think about that?"

And if you're reading this book, you have your perfect entry point. "I'm reading a book right now, and one of the assignments is to go to my partner and ask how they feel about monogamy. So...what are your thoughts?"

From there, you can use the five Ws to start getting curious and see where your partner's at. And in all likelihood, your partner will turn the question on you and ask your thoughts. This is the launchpad for the conversation, not the end of it. Because if there's one thing you'll soon discover as you begin practicing ENM, it's that you have to communicate, communicate, communicate.

My partner and I have been ENM since day one, but what that looks like for us has changed as our relationship—and the world around us—changes. At the time the pandemic lockdown hit, we were in a monogamish relationship with a DADT policy and had never played together with a third party. I requested that we close up the relationship during that time. "The world feels really unsafe, and while I know you literally can't go out and hook up with anyone else, I would ask that we don't do any flirting or anything else online either." We both understood this was a temporary arrangement based on unprecedented circumstances, and he was completely on board.

And as we neared the eighth month of lockdown, I saw there could be another way. I signed us up for a couples dating profile on Feeld, and we began playing with other women who'd been diligent about COVID safety.

Then the world opened back up, albeit slowly. And as my partner prepared to go on a trip alone, I knew it was time to have the conversation again. "Let's talk about how we want things to look moving forward."

As I write this, we're in a place in our relationship where we're dating other humans separately and together, with agreed-upon boundaries and best practices. And while—to an outsider—our relationship structure looks a heck of a lot like "hierarchical poly," we're not rushing to affix labels to our practice.

By the time you read this, though, our relationship may look vastly different. Or it might not. Humans evolve. Our needs evolve. Our relationships evolve. I can't predict what the future will look like, but I do know we'll be having plenty of conversations about how ENM works for us, and making adjustments as needed.

"But, Rena. What about jealousy?" you might be wondering.

Oh yes. Of course.

Rates of jealousy aren't any higher in ENM relationships than monogamous ones.

For the people in the back:

Rates of jealousy aren't any higher in ENM relationships than monogamous ones.

Before I jump into what jealousy *is*, let's explore what jealousy *isn't*.

I often hear folks using the term *jealousy* when, in fact, they mean *envy*. Envy refers to wanting what someone else has.

Salivating over the delicious restaurant pic your best friend posted online and wishing you were eating the same dish? That's envy. You want what they're having.

But what if that same friend posted a restaurant photo of them with their arms around another pal with the caption "best friends forever"? You might be a bit miffed, and *that* feeling is called jealousy. You're scared of losing a valuable part of a relationship you're already in.

Jealousy always involves a rival; envy doesn't. And this rival doesn't have to be an actual human. Maybe your partner has taken up rock climbing on weekends, and it's eating into your rare quality time together. Even if you have zero desire whatsoever to rock climb (i.e., you're not *envious*), you might feel *jealous* because your partner is choosing rock climbing over *you*.

When it comes to romance, being in a monogamous relationship doesn't shield you from feeling jealous. And being ENM doesn't automatically mean that you don't feel jealousy either. We *all* occasionally feel insecure or competitive in our relationships, no matter how they're structured. Because open communication is so critical in ENM relationships, though, people tend to talk about and process their jealousy more openly.‡

So how do you manage it? Get curious about how you're feeling and figure out what the story is you're telling yourself. Then express that to your partner. This can look like "I felt angry when I saw you talking to that other woman at the bar and didn't introduce me. The story I'm telling myself is that you wanted her to think you were single, and that made me feel jealous."

Obviously, the specifics will vary depending on what your relationship configuration is. But the "I felt sad/angry/scared when [specific instance]. The story I'm telling myself is [what your fears are], and that made me feel jealous" is the simplest framework to use to get the discussion started. This will provide you and your partner an open space to dig below the emotion and truly figure out what's going on. In the above example at the bar, it could be you're scared they will leave you for someone else. But maybe it was that your partner took someone else on a date to the exact restaurant you've been dying to try. You could feel sad or angry because your interests feel unheard.

Because you're allowed to design your own ground rules and frameworks within ENM, these feelings of jealousy can provide a great opportunity to request some modifications:

---

‡ When it comes to threesomes and group sex, jealousy tends to behave a little differently. I'll be diving more into that particular breed of the green-eyed monster in Lesson 25, "Make It a Group Thing."

- I know it's natural for you to flirt with other people, but I'd prefer not to see it. Maybe when we're out together, we keep our focus on each other?
- I'm okay with you taking other people on dates, but if it's a spot you know I've been wanting to check out, can we go there together first?

Keep in mind: these are requests, and your partner is allowed to say no. If you find you're constantly dodging jealousy land mines because of your ENM configuration, figure out whether you can *both* get on board to modify what your arrangement looks like. And if you can't? Perhaps this isn't a fuck yes relationship—and you know what to do if that's the case!

Does the fact that you're jealous mean you're *bad* at ENM? Not necessarily. Monogamous relationships end all the time because of incompatibility, and we don't say it's because we're bad at monogamy. ENM relationships are no different. It could be that this particular form of ENM with this specific person wasn't the right fit. Be curious about other possibilities!

But say you've reached the end of this chapter thinking, "Nope, Rena. I'm good with monogamy!" That's perfectly great. You've examined your default setting, and it works for you! The key here is *knowing* you have the power to switch it at any time.

15

Go with the Flow

Up until now, you've read stories of women all across the wide sexuality spectrum. I haven't made it a point to distinguish between straight and queer women, because their sexual orientation hasn't made much of a difference in terms of how intimacy struggles show up or how to resolve them.

There's one exception to that rule of thumb: with women who are attracted to other women but who have very little experience acting on their attractions. I used to be one of those women. My clients—and the data—suggest we're more common than you might think. So I'm creating an entire chapter to talk about what you'll come to realize is a blind spot in terms of broader conversations we're having about sexual attractions and desires.

Even though I've been sexually attracted to women for as long as I can remember, I didn't identify anything other than "straight" until a few years ago.

Sure, I had my fair share of playing doctor with my girlfriends in elementary school. I gravitated toward girl-on-girl porn as soon as I was aware that was a thing. As a teen, I had a few three-somes with whatever boyfriend I had at the time and whichever female friend happened to be down for it.

I chalked those experiences up to young experimentation. Nothing too crazy or outside the lines.

With men, there was always the sense I was building some-thing (even if that something ended up crumbling to the ground); with women, it felt like we were indulging. Indulging in curi-osity. Indulging in the thing that happens after one too many drinks. Indulging in a part of us that finds women to be beautiful creatures—and, in some ways, reminding me that I am also a beautiful creature.

A few years ago, I recorded a female sexual fluidity tutorial with a colleague of mine who identifies as a queer woman. As we began rolling, I confessed to her that I didn't consider myself to be bisexual because I don't date women in the same way I date men.

"I don't want to appropriate what it means to be a 'real' bisex-ual," I explained, "even though I'm just as sexually attracted to women as I am to men."

She offered me a reframe: "What if you were to see bisexuality as an umbrella?"

She explained that she considers herself to be bisexual, even though she couldn't see herself being in a long-term relationship with a cisgender man ever again.

"What if what you're describing *is* bisexual, and bisexuality is more nuanced than this black-or-white thing?"

Intellectually, that made sense to me. Yes, I am a person who is attracted sexually to more than one gender. No, I'm not attracted to them in quite the same way. And that's still enough to be bisexual (at least as far as she was concerned).

But that didn't help me feel like less of an impostor at the time. Sure, I'd had sex with women before. I knew *how* to. But did I feel like I could walk into a queer bar and belong? Not then, I didn't.

Which is why Skirt Club appealed to me. Founded in London in 2014, Skirt Club has since evolved into an international network of events that provide a "safe space for bi-curious and bisexual women." Women who want to play with each other far away from the male gaze. I applied for membership and was quickly accepted.

Most of the articles I'd read about Skirt Club described debaucherous nights of orgies and in-your-face sexuality. Their Instagram account frequently features "lost and found" posts of items women had left behind at parties: designer panties, jewelry, elaborate angel wings.

I quickly learned that Skirt Club hosts a range of events and that their "Signature parties" (described above) weren't the standard. I purchased a ticket for "Mini Skirt": a shorter, tamer evening. It was clear this wouldn't be a full-blown sex party, but it was completely unclear what it *would* be.

As it turned out, it was body shots. Spin the bottle. A burlesque performer who lost both of her pasties during the performance (and a wave of "Wooooo!" from the dozens of women surrounding her as it happened).

"This is like a bachelorette party meets a slumber party," I whispered to Kiki, my ally for the night. We'd met during an icebreaker, both of us carrying matching playing cards that had been distributed to each woman who entered the bar. (It turns out "First four women to find their match get a tequila shot!" is a great way to get strangers to start talking to each other.)

In addition to the playing cards, first-timers were also given a black ribbon with a small charm in the shape of a key to wear around our wrists. "So you'll know who the other new people are," the hostess explained.

With our matching bracelets and playing cards, we set out to mingle with the others. I met lawyers and teachers and advertising executives and poets…and almost every woman I spoke to was married to a man.

Including Kiki. She and her husband had opened up their marriage a few months beforehand.

"I met a dom and have gotten into BDSM recently. I *love* being a submissive!" Our journeys had followed similar arcs, and it warmed my heart. I liked her.

And then she kissed me, which I wasn't expecting. That kiss turned into a make-out—the least G-rated that'd happened at the event.

"I want you to bite my tits," she whispered into my ear, "right now."

I obliged, only slightly caring that we were on full display in a bar full of dozens of women.

And then she left to fuck a guy she'd started dating.

"Let me know when you're free this week to get together!" She smiled and kissed me on the cheek on her way out. The party dwindled, and women began congregating on the sidewalk, plotting their next move. Would they hit a bar up the street? Go back to someone's hotel room?

"Wait. Where did your friend go?" they asked me, seemingly in unison, as I called an Uber.

"Oh, Kiki! Yeah, she went to get some dick."

Their faces fell immediately.

Do I have dogshit all over me? Why are they giving me that look?

"Girl, I'm sorry," an Amazonian blond in a micro sequin dress said, patting my shoulder. "That's not fucking cool."

Beside her, another one chimed in, outraged, "Girl, what the hell? You two were, like, making out just now! And then she ditched you?"

My brain did not compute.

Until it did.

They weren't being judgmental; they were being *sisters*.

These women had one night to do this. An evening of freedom. A sexual hall pass until they turned into dick-loving, married pumpkins at midnight. They didn't want me to waste my "limited" exploration time on a dead end.

Some had flown in from other parts of the state to be there. Others had made the drive from Orange County (which may as well be another state) into West Hollywood. And while I was absolutely cursing having to take an Uber from Echo Park down the Sunset Strip on a Friday evening, tonight was the beginning of a story for me, not the entirety of it.

Having now been to several Skirt Club parties, I can't say those ladies were the typical crowd. In fact, I can't say there *is* a typical crowd. Yes, they're all bisexual or "bi-curious" women. Some are the leggy model types who feature prominently in their marketing (branding so strong that I questioned whether I'd even be granted membership when I applied). But I've also seen women in their fifties sporting leather harnesses. Plus-sized women walking around a penthouse rooftop completely naked. Women of all races and colors. Artists alongside surgeons. Women who've never kissed a woman and women who'd only recently started sleeping with men.

It's a diverse space. It's a unique space. *It's a necessary space.*

Most play parties are co-ed, male only, or—if they're geared solely toward women—are BDSM and kink oriented. Lesbian and queer bars have closed at a staggering rate over the last thirty years. (Although, in the time it took me to write this book, two new ones have opened up in LA, so perhaps the pendulum is starting to swing!)

At the same time, women are becoming *more* sexually fluid. Year after year, we're reporting more same-sex attraction than men (whose heterosexuality rates have remained pretty constant). In 2019, only 65 percent of women reported being attracted only to men!

What does this mean? It means there's a decent likelihood that you've either been with women or want to. And it also means there's a decent chance you're struggling to figure out how to do it. As someone who had slept with women but still felt like an impostor the handful of times I'd gone to queer bars or clubs, I'm speaking to the women out there who have fantasies and curiosities you simply don't know how to indulge in.

My client Julie was one of those women. She's in her late forties, divorced, and has had her fair share of threesomes (usually spontaneous hookups spawned in luxury hotel lobbies during work travel).

"I want to play with women on my own," she told me, "but I just don't feel like I'm queer enough to pass as queer."

She lives in Brooklyn, with a fair share of gay, lesbian, and bisexual friends. Still, she felt like she'd be playing tourist if she asked them for help.

"Why would a queer woman want to hook up with *me*?" she asked. "I don't even really know what I'm doing!"

I remembered back to another client, Savannah, who's a lesbian. She'd written "Be a bi-curious woman's first" on her 27 Things list. When I'd asked her to elaborate, she told me that being able to truly help a woman explore her body and desires would be both an honor and a complete turn-on. "Who wouldn't want to give someone an amazing queer experience?"

I gave Julie the reframe, assuring her it came from a real-life lesbian woman and not some hypothetical pie-in-the-sky idea I had formulated as her coach.

"Don't pretend to be someone you're not," I reminded her. "Go on the apps. Be honest about your experience and lack of experience and how you're looking to explore. Sure, some women will be turned away by it. But some women will be turned *on* by it."

I've also worked with clients who have absolutely zero sexual experience with women, and about half of them express some interest in doing so in their list of 27 Things.

If you, like any of these women, are curious to indulge, start by asking yourself some questions.

Is this something you want to do solo with another solo woman or in the context of a threesome or moresome? Are you looking to play with your partner and another woman? Are you looking to be a unicorn (the single woman who joins another couple)? Write. It. Down.

If you're looking for a group setting, I recommend the dating app Feeld to get started. Feeld was originally called 3nder when it was created in 2014 (they changed their name in 2016 after being sued by Tinder) with the goal of connecting people looking to explore outside the box of conventional monogamy. It has since branched out to include pretty much anything you can think of outside the hetero-mono-vanilla-normative box but remains the biggest app for those looking for threesomes or moresomes.

Feeld is also a fantastic jumping-off point if you're looking to explore solo with another woman, as is an app called Her. Mainstream dating sites such as Tinder, Match, Bumble, and Hinge are also perfectly fine to use, though I've heard from women anecdotally they receive more unsolicited messages from men on those apps, even when they've specifically said they're only looking to meet women.

Regardless of the app you choose, be honest. If you have zero experience with women and are looking to explore but take things slowly, say that. If you're looking to have an experience with a couple, say that. If you've explored lightly with women before but want to take it to the next level, say that. Based on the statistics I cited earlier, there are plenty of women in your shoes.

And if you happen to live close to a city with a Skirt Club chapter, apply for membership. They're constantly expanding their global presence, so even if there isn't a party you can attend in-person right now, there are virtual mixers and orientations at your disposal.

So you might be thinking "But what the hell do I do once I've met a woman?!" And that's a valid question, one I hear often from women at the early stages of their exploration. If you're looking for some guidance on female pleasure, I recommend the following books as a starting point:

- *She Comes First* by Ian Kerner
- *Becoming Cliterate* by Laurie Mintz
- *Girl Sex 101* by Allison Moon, illustrated by kd diamond

I'm going to add a massive caveat here though: women don't actually come with an instruction manual. You can read all the books I mentioned above, but your intuition is your best guide. Not all of us like to be touched the same way or on the same parts of our bodies. And not all women have vulvas, or want theirs to be touched. I once slept with a lesbian woman who identifies as a "stone butch," who kept her clothes on the entire time we were in bed together. Her breasts and genitals were off limits, and she derived sexual pleasure from touching me (not the other way around). Some trans women don't have vulvas, and there's a wide spectrum of the type of touch they want below the waist. I've been with trans women who've said, "You can treat this body part like a penis," and some who've asked me to handle their genitals more like large clitorises. Some have expressed that any touch below the waist makes them feel masculinized/defeminized (and requested that I ignore that region entirely) while others have enthusiastically consented to a variety of play and sensations.

In short: regardless of anyone's gender or sexual identity, don't make assumptions when it comes to body boundaries. "How do you like to be touched?" and "Do you have any body boundaries?" are great places to start when it comes to any sexual partner, whether they identify as female, male, or non-binary.

Also understand, not all of us are able to orgasm the same way. Sure, there are some general statistics about how women with vulvas orgasm (mostly through external clitoral stimulation), but the best way to give pleasure to another human being is to *ask* what they like!

And you have a real advantage here, being a woman yourself. I've been with women who'd never had a bisexual experience before and lesbian women who've slept with women their entire lives. And I'll tell you this: I've noticed almost no difference insofar as "skill" level is concerned. In fact, the best female lover I've ever had was someone just like me: she'd had a few hookups but not nearly as much sex as she'd had with men. Because skill level and pleasure are very subjective, there's no way research could encompass the wide range of what women consider to be "good in bed" when it comes to other women. But the research *does* tell us that "women have more orgasms when they have sex with other women than when they have sex with men...because having a clitoris teaches you that it's important to ask a partner just how *hers* needs to be stimulated."

As with a lot of my advice, it all comes back around to communication. Ask her preferences, and be ready to share your own, both when you're trying to meet someone and when you make it to the bedroom. Get some data beforehand as to what she wants or is curious to try. Also ask if there are any no-go areas. Check in during the experience with questions like "Do you like this?" "Harder or softer?" "Is this okay?"

Most importantly: *Enjoy yourself.* Be fluid. Be open. Be curious. Have fun!

16

Get Creative

T his is your worst relationship nightmare come true," said my therapist during the first of many virtual sessions we had during the pandemic.

Since day one, my partner and I have built a relationship that prides itself on trying new things, having new experiences—not being *lazy* when it comes to our quality time. For the first six months we were together, we made it a point to never visit the same bar or restaurant twice. We took turns planning dates. We were detectives, constantly on the hunt for some new way to bring fun and joy into our relationship.

On a personal level, this wasn't just about excitement and adventure though. This was a heart-shaped cross I bore: learn from your past relationship mistakes, or you'll be doomed to repeat them. Routines—how we live, what we do, how we love—are easy to slip into. Based on my track record, I'd made a commitment to avoid routines at all cost, a firm resolve to not become a—shudder—Netflix and chill couple. And my therapist knew this.

Then a global pandemic hit. We were forced into lockdown. One by one, I began deleting all the upcoming events on my calendar (bye-bye, *Book of Mormon* and Magic Castle; so long, Mexico and Iceland!). Each domino of fun and excitement came tumbling down.

How would a relationship built on variety and novelty survive this type of reckoning? The "Remember when my biggest worry in life was becoming a Netflix and chill couple?" texts went from ending with a crying laughing emoji to just a crying emoji. This relationship—this beautiful, living, unconventional structure—was something we had built from the ground up. And it was on fire.

The problem was *the entire world was on fire*, and there was little anyone could do about it. Or was there? Someone much wiser than me must have the answer, right?

Viktor Frankl once said, "When we are no longer able to change a situation, we are challenged to change ourselves." I couldn't change the external world, but I could reframe the way I—and my relationship—existed in it.

Positive psychology tells us that a key to well-being is using the strengths we already have at our disposal. In reflecting, I realized a core strength of our relationship had been creativity, not novelty. It was receiving a text that said "Be at my place at 7:00. Wear something warm." It was going to some unique event, then saying, "Thank you so much for finding this for us." It was giving each other greeting cards for no reason other than to say I love you.

With a nonexistent social calendar staring us in the face, I realized the same creativity that had been the cornerstone of building our partnership was the one strength we could rely on to maintain it. Just because we couldn't go into the world for dates didn't mean we couldn't *date*.

So we did as we had done in "the before" and took turns planning our time together in the most imaginative ways we could:

- I organized a tiki night: a talented bartender friend (who was out of work due to COVID closures) delivered mai tai ingredients and mixing instructions curbside; I foraged the neighborhood for flowers and made a tropical centerpiece; we dressed up in our best tiki attire, ate pupus, and watched *Blue Hawaii*.
- We made each other special anagrams and crossword puzzles (with a prize at the end, of course).
- I scoured the web for ways to bring outside world entertainment into my home. We streamed live comedy shows, live magic shows, even a live candlelight classical concert (which, incidentally, had been the last live performance we went to before COVID hit). For the latter, he wore a suit and alternated between being "our" waiter and being my date while presenting each dinner course.
- Like every other person during quarantine, I baked sourdough bread. Instead of making artisanal boule after boule, I'd ask him for special requests. "Rosemary olive sourdough focaccia? Sure!"
- He invited me over for "wine and pizza" one Sunday night and opened the door wearing a bathrobe and face covering

(no wine or pizza in sight). "Oh. You must be Rena with the 6:00 massage appointment?" He led me into the bedroom, which he'd set up as a "spa." Not breaking character, he asked me to undress and get below the sheet and told me he'd be back in a few minutes. (He even asked if I'd like some water—bless!) I got an amazing massage and…I'll leave it up to you to insert whatever "happy ending" joke you'd like at this point.

• Frequently, we'd order in dinner and pick a movie to corre- spond to the meal or vice versa. If we were feeling a little "extra," we'd throw on a Spotify playlist tying into the eve- ning's theme. (Which is how I discovered there's a "Pizza" playlist on there, and it's awesomely terrible.)

None of these dates took much money; what they took was an intention to make things special. When you treat your quality time with your partner as a craft—one to hone, add flair to, make uniquely your own—you tap into an entirely new love language: creativity.

When you set creativity as your intention, you create a small change that becomes a world of difference. It's the difference between letting Netflix be the *center* of your quality time and finding ways to incorporate Netflix *into* your quality time. It's the difference between opening up a box of crackers to offer some to your partner as a "snack" before dinner and arranging some of them on a plate, throwing on some cheese, and calling it an "aperitivo." It's the difference between asking "What should we order tonight?" and planning it earlier and pairing a movie with it. It's the difference between "hanging out" and "dating."

For me, it was the difference between my "worst relationship nightmare come true" and a chance to redefine what romance can be at any point in a relationship. It became a glimpse into the future, one that exists on a hammock swing on the porch, devoid of the entertainment dedicated to a younger generation. It became a chance to see what love can be as it spans into the cosmos of a world we have not yet envisioned. It became a sense of hope—hope of how resilient our capacity is to love, be loved, and make love. It became a crisp, blank canvas on which we were beckoned to create our masterpiece.

Lockdowns are over (is it jinxing something to type that?), and we're now a few more years into our relationship (the "comfort stage," as many people would call it). I'm no longer employed by the county with a clock-in/clock-out cadence to my days. Being my own boss has tons of advantages, don't get me wrong: I can schedule my workouts when I want to. I can clear my calendar for days (like this) to sit down and write.

But having agency over my time—coupled with being in the "comfort stage" of my relationship—means I have to make a deliberate attempt to not let things grow stale.

In Lesson 11, "If It's Not a Fuck Yes, It's a No," I called bullshit on the idea that relationships are supposed to be hard. But I firmly believe *relationships take work*. The good news is it's fun work that doesn't actually feel like work. So perhaps I'm saying instead: relationships take effort.

You may have heard of the 5 Love Languages. Coined by Gary Chapman (and written about at length in a book under the same name), the concept tells us there are five (admittedly unscientific) "languages" when it comes to expressing love:

1. Physical touch
2. Quality time
3. Words of affirmation
4. Gifts
5. Acts of service

The idea is that each of us has a preferred way (or ways) we like to give and receive love. But our partner's language(s) may be completely different. Our wires can become crossed. We may feel like they don't love us because they're not expressing love in the way *we* want to hear it.

Words of affirmation are huge to me. I like to be told I'm loved. I'm pretty. I'm smart and interesting and kind and…all the things. My ex's love language was acts of service, typically in the form of spreadsheets and Trello boards. He project managed our relationship. Not only did that drive me absolutely insane, but it left me feeling unseen and uncared for. It wasn't that he didn't love me; it's that he wasn't speaking my language.

My client Mariam was in a similar mismatched dilemma, which she became acutely aware of when she got home from a business trip.

"He cleaned the entire house and did all the laundry so I wouldn't have anything to do when I got home. But he didn't respond to a single text message I'd sent him that day." The next night, she reminded him that her love language is words of affirmation rather than acts of service. "He was vulnerable and told me that doing things for me is easier than saying things."

She opened up to him. He opened up to her. But then he leaned into his own discomfort.

"This morning, he left me a note before leaving for work. He wrote out all the reasons I'm a great wife and mom. He'd never done anything like that before, and it meant the world to me." And—news flash!—writing a note takes a hell of a lot less time than doing all the laundry.

If you're in a relationship where your languages are mismatched, it doesn't signal the end. But you have to let each other know what your respective language are *and* how you want to receive love in those languages.§ Do you prefer a massage to a cuddle on the couch? Would you rather have a sweet text every day or be surprised with a card for no reason? Yes, there are different love languages, but within each category, there's an infinite number of ways we prefer to be spoken to. So get clear. Your partner doesn't have a crystal ball. Tell them how you want to be loved.

Here's the catch though: don't do the same shit all the time. *Get creative.* Think of creativity as an accent or dialect; it's not a love language in and of itself, but it's a way you "speak" in each language. Imagine love itself as a coloring book: your partner's love language is the black outlines, and the colors to fill them in are your creativity.

So for example, I'm big on words of affirmation. An ex-boyfriend of mine used to text me out of the blue with "You're so pretty" or "I love you." Which was sweet. The problem arose when those were the *only* ways he'd express love in my language. Day after day, he alternated between those two texts. The words became white noise in our relationship rather than a symphony.

---

§ If you don't know your love languages, you can take a quiz online at www.5lovelanguages.com.

There was effort but no creativity. Mexican might be your favorite type of food, but you don't want your partner to cook you tacos every single day, do you?

My current partner, on the other hand, has a black belt in creativity. A few months into our relationship, I was heading on a solo trip to Mexico. I made a last-minute stop at Costco that morning and was rummaging in my purse to find my membership card so I wouldn't be the asshole who held up the line at the door. I found a postcard tucked in my purse—a photo by William Eggleston called *En Route to New Orleans* on one side, a handwritten note on the other. My partner had wished me a wonderful trip and told me he was grateful for the chance encounter that had led me into his life. "You are a lovely human being...and very...exciting. Never stop being you. I'll be thinking of you."

The postcard couldn't have cost more than a few dollars. It probably took him under five minutes to write the message on it. But it made me ugly cry in a Costco parking lot. That was the first of many, many times he's spoken to me in my language. One Valentine's Day, he wrote a few dozen love notes and hid them around my apartment (I'm still finding them, to this day). Every so often, I'll get a text from him that says "You're special because..." with a very specific reason as to why he loves me.

Part of what makes this expressions special is the *fact* they're different each time. You can love creatively, or you can love lazily. This is the relationship version of planning different activities for your kids versus leaving them with an iPad twenty-four seven. Relationships take effort, yes. But as you can see from the above examples, the effort doesn't have to be expensive or time consuming.

I started this lesson talking about how to date mindfully and warned of the perils of falling into routines. But routines do have some value. Most days, I wake up, feed my cat, then boil water for my coffee (yes, I drink instant coffee—judge me all you want). While the water boils, I make my bed and clear up anything I was too lazy to put away the night before. I pour my coffee and sit down to journal.

Same shit most days, which I'm perfectly fine with. The energy I don't expend trying to come up with a creative way to drink my coffee is mental bandwidth I can use in other (more important) areas of my life. That's the value of routines: they free up space to give more fucks about the important things in life.

Like relationships.

So yes, routines have their place, but too much routine in a relationship will still kill the romantic spark.

"But, Rena. I don't have time to come up with fancy new date ideas every week!" you might think as you roll your eyes.

Here's where rituals come in.

The difference between a routine and a ritual is the intention behind it. Routine is autopilot; ritual is a framework.

For example, I have a "100 Greatest Films of All Time" scratch-off poster hanging on my wall. On Monday nights, my partner comes over. I cook dinner, and we abstain from drinking any alcohol. We alternate picking a movie off the poster. We then start the movie. Inevitably he ends up cocooned on the couch in every single throw blanket I own. One of us will get up multiple times to grab my cat and bring him over to said couch to snuggle, which'll last approximately thirty seconds. Once the movie ends, I'll scratch it off the poster while he looks up fun trivia on IMDb and reads it out loud to me.

We've scratched about seventy-five movies off the poster. That's a lot of Mondays doing the same shit...where it's never the same exact shit.

Think of the thing you'd like to do more of in your relationship, and then come up with an easy-to-remember structure to implement it. This doesn't have to be rocket science.

Maybe you buy a cookbook and take turns making a new recipe together every Wednesday. Or every other Friday is "date night" and you alternate who plans the date. Maybe you have Taco Tuesdays at home, but you make it a point to look up a different taco recipe each week. No matter what it is, pick something with a little structure and plenty of room for improvisation.

Like your partner's love language, a ritual gives you a set of outlines to fill in however you want.

Creativity is one of the most valuable relationship tools at your disposal. So pick up that brush and start splashing some color into yours!

17

Give It Room to Breathe

sit here typing from a lodge in the woods in Idyllwild, a small mountain town a few hours outside LA that happens to be my "happy place." I'm here solo for four nights. Away from the distractions of home. But also away from my partner.

He's going on his own four-night getaway to work on music next week at a different cabin in a different mountain town a few hours outside LA.

Would it make more sense from a logistical and economic standpoint for us to have rented a big house and done our work together? Obviously, yes.

But it wouldn't have served its purpose. He and I both need to be in flow state in order to perfect our craft, and we've found it's damn near impossible to do that if we're within breathing room of each other. Even if we could focus around each other, though, I wouldn't want to sacrifice this trip by myself.

If I were traveling with my partner, I would've missed out on the drive I made up here. A drive where I chose to listen to a nostalgic Spotify playlist instead of podcasts. A playlist that took me back to times and lovers past. To heartbreak and inner turmoil. Each song was a form of the gratitude I feel today for being able to speak freely and clearly and finally feel safe to be myself. I cried unattractively, which I wouldn't have done had my partner and I been chatting alongside each other in the car. I needed that space to tap into my emotions again. To remind me of where I was. To juxtapose the drives I used to make up to this tiny mountain town every year with my ex-husband and the tears I would shed into my late-night whiskey while sitting alone on the deck of whatever Airbnb we'd happened to rent.

I'd also have missed out on bizarre human connections. If you ever want people to make conversation with you while you're alone, sit down at the bar area of a restaurant and bring a book to read. People find a way to ask what you're reading, why you're there—*what your story is*—in a way that simply doesn't happen when you're out with your partner. It's a reminder that you are someone. That you have a story that sits on its own. When "Are you *two* from around here?" isn't an option, people can't be as conversationally lazy.

While sipping wine and eating ragù fettuccine last night, I met a lively pair of married men in their fifties.

"I studied literature in college," one of them remarked after asking about the book I was reading.

"And now he's a girls' lacrosse coach," the other one piped in.

"It's a good thing I'm not a sex crimes DA anymore. I prosecuted way too many girls' fill-in-the-blank coaches that I'm a bit jaded," I joked.

"Oh, well, that's just something I do on the side. My main job is selling ice cream."

The joke wrote itself, but I bit my tongue. It was exactly the sort of interaction I cherish when I'm out alone.

As psychotherapist Esther Perel says, "Fire needs air. Desire needs space."

Or, as a dear friend of mine says, "How can I miss you if you won't go away?"

What both boil down to is the need to have time apart. To maintain your own separate sense of self in a relationship in order for the relationship itself to survive.

Which is the same reason that—after half a decade—my partner and I don't live together but around the corner from each other. (If you've ever seen a pink-haired woman with a cat strapped to her back in a pet carrier walking up a hill, that'd be me!) Again, logistically and economically, it would "make sense" for us to move in together, but it might cost us our relationship if we did.

People ask me frequently whether he and I will get married. You might think I'd answer a resounding "hell no" after the tales I've shared with you so far about my experiences with marriage.

Instead, I normally say, "I'd marry him tomorrow if we could still live separately."

And then people ask what the point of that would be. And I don't quite have an answer for them.

There's this idea that two people will meet. They'll date. They'll fall in love. They'll move in together. Get married. Have kids. They'll hop right on "the relationship escalator," as I've called it elsewhere in this book.

What most people don't see is that there are lots of ways to the top. You can take the stairs. You can change your mind halfway through and decide you're fine on this particular floor. You can exit the building and find an untouched path that leads you to your destination. You don't have to race to marriage and kids to prove you're in love.

Too often, though, we hop on the escalator in the honeymoon stage (where, consciously or not, we have the most breathing room) without much thought.

"Everything's going great! Let's keep going!" we say and hurry on. Then, by the time we get to the top, we've catapulted the partnership into a space with no breathing room at all.

As someone who always made major life decisions (e.g., moving in) within the honeymoon stage, I'm here to say: don't do that. Just like you wouldn't make huge financial decisions if you've had one too many drinks, don't write an emotional check when you're drunk on love.

But say you've passed that point. You've moved in together. Maybe you're married and you have kids and this is the life that resonates with you. Not everyone wants or is able to live around the corner from their partner like I do after all. How, then, do you give your relationship that oxygen injection it needs for the fire to keep burning?

For one, schedule date nights...apart. Yes, you heard me. Everyone talks about couples (especially those with kids) needing to schedule date nights. What I've seen often, though, is the date nights together end up becoming a way to talk about the kids without the kids there to bug you. The fancy restaurant becomes your kitchen table, just in a different kitchen.

The purpose of having solo date nights is to remember who you were before you became a parent or unit. So sit down with your partner, decide how often you can commit to giving each other a solo night, and then take turns (biweekly or monthly is a great frequency). And you can use your date time however the hell you please. You want to go dancing with your friends? Great. Get stoned and play video games in the basement? Have at it. Go to the movies and watch the exact film genre your partner hates? Perfect.

And yes, do plan date nights together. But get ready for them separately. Have a grand reveal. Meet at the restaurant if you can...or even in the car or at the front door.

Don't underestimate the power of mystery. Growing up, I watched my mom have full-blown conversations with my dad while he was on the toilet. Every morning, he'd sit on his porcelain throne for about an hour, *Los Angeles Times* in hand. He isn't a big coffee or breakfast person, so this was how they'd communicate. I remember thinking to myself, "Wow. I guess love means you're so comfortable with another person you're totally okay taking a shit in front of them."

Please, don't do that. Yes, we're all humans who piss and shit and fart and burp, and there's no shame in how our bodies work. But at the same time, leave some mystery there.

My client Aria and her husband had been peeing with the door open their entire seven-year relationship. And they were paying the price for it: they were like two planets, their home merely a solar system in which they orbited. Once they started closing the actual bathroom door, a larger proverbial door opened: one where they could start seeing each other as objects of desire rather than mere humans who shared a space.

Interestingly, Aria and her husband also slept in separate bedrooms.

"I'm guessing you're going to say that's a bad idea, right?"

Wrong.

I say, "Having separate bedrooms is a fantastic idea so long as you're mindful about it."

What I mean is are you using the separate bedrooms as a way to *escape each other* or as a way to *find yourself*?

You'll hear folks saying, "My parents didn't even sleep in the same bed" as though it's a bad thing. As though the only way two people will ever have sex is if they share a bed all the time. And that line of thinking perpetuates this notion that there is only one time of day to get intimate and only one place to do it. But as we're learning, there are as many times and places to get sexy as there are people looking to do so. In fact, I would argue that having separate bedrooms can make the art of seduction easier.

"Hey, wanna come into my room for a bit?" is a bit cheeky, right?

I'm actually seeing more and more younger couples moving into two- (or more) bedroom houses or apartments and *choosing* to have separate living quarters. They can decorate their rooms as they want. They can sleep together if they choose or not. If one's a night owl and the other one's an early bird, no one has to compromise. (And no one gets woken up by snoring!)

"Wait, Rena. Doesn't that mean they're just roommates?"

It could devolve into that, yes. But so can *any* relationship, even one where folks sleep in the same bed every night. (I'll be touching on this idea more in Lesson 20, "Schedule It.") Your relationship's strength is based on your actions, not your bed arrangement.

Sometimes it takes an unexpected tragedy to shine a light on how enmeshed we've become with our partner. Yes, there's the archetype of the widow who no longer knows who she is after her husband's sudden passing. She has no air pockets of her own and is reminded of him during all her activities. But sometimes that tragedy comes in the form of a betrayal, as was the case with my client Raven.

Raven and her husband had been together for about a decade when she came to me. They're successful business owners and live in a beautiful home in the suburbs of the Bay Area of California together with their daughter. They maintain a fun social life aside from their roles as parents, making trips into the city to go clubbing with friends. While they're doing the whole parenting thing right, they've also not lost sight of the joie de vivre they had before their daughter came around. Being parents doesn't define them.

Sounds great, right? Yes. Life was great. Until Raven found out her husband had been cheating on her for the last two years in a string of casual hookups with men.

"I had no idea he was bisexual. None. The betrayal hurts of course, but not as much as him feeling like he couldn't feel safe to tell me that he wants to be with men too."

They'd been in couples therapy to process the infidelity and what it would mean for the future of their relationship. Raven wanted to stay married and was willing to accommodate an open arrangement that would allow her husband to feel sexually fulfilled without the shame of sneaking around.

Her husband has always been the bright star in the room, the life of the party. She was the more tempered one, who felt like she had to keep it all together. Once her husband came out as bisexual, she went with him to gay clubs, excited to see him flourishing in his element, while she felt like the camp counselor who was overseeing the kids while they had fun.

"I see my husband being light when we're at the clubs together. It's hard for me to find that carefree space. I don't allow myself to have an outlet."

She didn't want to be a wallflower anymore, letting her husband suck all the air out of the room and their relationship. He was only the second sexual partner she'd ever had. And while she fully encouraged him to explore his sexuality, she realized she'd never been in touch with her own. "I've never felt comfortable in my body. I have no idea how to express my needs in the bedroom. I want to have *my* sexual awakening too. I want to give myself the freedoms I've never allowed myself to."

Pretty soon into our work together, Raven and her husband embarked on a preplanned road trip to Vegas to celebrate their anniversary. I suggested she download a conversation starter app and use it as a springboard to have an intimate dialogue during their long car ride. She had to answer questions about her wants and her needs—something she'd never given herself permission to do. And then something magical happened in Sin City.

During our initial consultation, Raven expressed that she'd love to feel confident in a bathing suit someday, and two weeks into our work together, she found herself topless at an adult pool at their Vegas hotel. "A woman started flirting with me. I'm not even sure I'm into women in that way, but it felt amazing to push outside my comfort zone. I felt *free*."

And that freedom followed her home. During their next night

out clubbing together, she decided she wanted to be a happy camper instead of a camp counselor. "I got all dolled up and took control of myself and my night while we were out with friends. Eighty-year-old badass Raven said, 'Fuck it! Go to the after party!' So we went and had a blast."

As with all my clients (and readers!), I assigned Raven to take an erotic photo. As someone who hadn't ever felt sexy in her body, posing in a sexually suggestive way didn't come naturally to her. She was surprised with the results. "I desired *myself* after taking the photo."

I've talked a lot about creating physical breathing room in relationships, but Raven didn't do that. The adventures she had out in the world were with her husband. The change happened when she stopped breathing down *his* neck and gave *herself* space to have her own identity. To be another star, shining bright in the room (or tits out at the Vegas pool!). All it took was a simple shift in perspective.

No matter what, don't be afraid to not spend every waking moment together, even when you're on vacation. Whether it's a two-night getaway or a ten-day trip overseas, schedule solo time. This can be as simple as spending an hour on your own at a coffee shop or taking a cooking class while your partner goes indoor rock-climbing. Time apart means separate adventures. And you know what that means? That you've already got tons to talk about when you reconvene later.

Any time you create distance in your relationship—whether at home or on a trip—you drop quarters in the conversational piggy bank. See your time apart as an investment!

PART 3

MAKE SEX FUN AGAIN

18

Get Out of Your Head

Brushing my teeth before bed used to make me feel like shit.
I'd do it way longer than I needed to in the hopes that my then partner would be asleep by the time I came into the bedroom.

You must have the cleanest teeth in LA, I thought to myself, staring at my reflection in the mirror. But also, *What the fuck is wrong with you that you're in your twenties and have no libido at all?*

I was accustomed to coming up with every excuse in the book to avoid sex. I was too tired. I was too stressed. I went so far as to order some natural pills on the internet that claimed they would boost my desire. They didn't work (shocker, I know), because the problem was my mindset.

A significant number of my clients can't get out of their heads during sex.

"I want to be present," they tell me.

"I don't want sex to feel like a chore."

Sometimes this happens because of past trauma, as I discussed earlier in the book. In those instances, the body will dissociate because it's trying to protect you from an act it once perceived as dangerous.

But sometimes it's anything (and everything) else that takes us out of the moment. This lesson is here to address the elephant in the room. The voice in your head. The one that reminds you of every single item on your to-do list. The one that's looking at the clock, already worrying about your meeting tomorrow morning. The one that's criticizing your sagging breasts or postpartum belly. The one that might be saying, "Ugh, when will this be *over*?"

She's a loud bitch, that one. Her cries drown out every ounce of pleasure. She's the piece of food stuck in your molars after a meal, distracting you from conversation with friends. She's the chirp on your smoke alarm, begging for you to change its battery. She's the tiny pebble in your tennis shoe on your nature walk.

But *she is not you.*

Let that sink in. So much shame could be eliminated if we as women understood this simple fact. There's nothing wrong with you if your mind is wandering during sex, and there's more than one reason it might be happening.

We don't often complain about our minds wandering during a really intense workout or a delicious meal. We get really sucked in if we're watching an engaging movie, right? Maybe the reason your mind is wandering is that the sex itself isn't intense, delicious, or engaging. *Maybe your mind is wandering because the sex is boring.*

This isn't typically a *you* problem. It's a sex problem.

Let me illustrate by way of a thought experiment.

Think of a food you crave. It could be a hot bowl of ramen, some fresh sushi, a juicy burger. Whatever it is, imagine it. What does it look like? How does it smell? How does it feel in your mouth? How does the taste satiate you? Close your eyes right now and think about it. Imagine it. Taste it.

Then imagine ordering it for delivery to your home. Once you confirm the order, you spend the next hour or so anticipating its arrival, wanting it in your belly.

Now, bring yourself to the moment when your doorbell rings or your phone pings to let you know that your delicious meal has arrived.

You get the bag. You open the bag. And instead of that meal—whatever it is—you've imagined and anticipated, you see a 7-Eleven ham sandwich staring you in the face.

Bit of a letdown, huh?

When it comes to sex: What is that thing you're craving? What is the equivalent of the meal you wanted to be in that bag? What is that thing that you see in movies, that you hear a friend recounting a story about—the thing that makes you say, "That's fucking hot"? The thing you think about when you're pleasuring yourself? What is that?

And what is that thing that's in the bag, the thing you're getting? Are they the same?

For some of us, they might be. But for many women, they're worlds apart. And when you think about it that way, it's no wonder that you don't crave what's being offered to you, what's being presented to you, what's in the bag. We can't expect to crave a 7-Eleven ham sandwich, especially after daydreaming about sushi.

Put simply: *we can't expect to crave what we don't actually crave*. If the sex is boring, you're not going to want it. Period.

But what is boring? Is it missionary intercourse, lasting under a minute with him climaxing and you not? Is it you and your wife using the same toys in the same exact way, reaching the final goal of mutual orgasm but on the same worn path? Is it simply more of what you already do all the time, even if it's kinky as fuck?

Anything will become boring if it's on repeat. The meal you thought of earlier, the one you crave? You'd probably get sick of it if it were your only option for breakfast, lunch, and dinner. So not only do we need delicious sex, we need variety too.

Your mind will probably wander while you're driving to the same office every day or when you're making your coffee the way you always make it. Your mind will probably wander if you're seeing the same commercial for the tenth time or reading your kid the same bedtime story for (what feels like) the hundredth time.

Similarly, if your sex life is on autopilot—if it becomes routine—your mind is going to wander.

Here's the deal: you probably know what to do when you become bored in other areas of your life. If you're sick of the cafeteria food at your office, you might walk somewhere for lunch. If you're falling asleep every time you pick up the novel you've been "trying" to finish for six months, you might eventually shelve it for another book.

Your sex life is no different, friends.

You've already learned the value of creativity in your relationship; your bedroom *is* a part of your relationship.

But say you're in a rut. You know something needs to change, but you're not sure *what* or *how*? Don't worry: I'll be giving you some concrete options in the next few lessons.

For the time being, though, let's focus on your mindset. Let's get you thinking of the type of sex that you want.

Start by writing it out as an erotic short story. What *was* the sexual version of what you wish was in the takeout bag?

If your mind is blank, go back to the 27 Things list you created at the very beginning of your journey reading this book. Read through it. Feel it. Then put it away and sit (or lie) comfortably with your eyes closed. Let your imagination chew on it and start projecting your list in your mind's eye like a movie. You're visualizing the life you want. Now, ask yourself: what would a sex scene in this movie look like?

Open your eyes, and start writing. Aim for two hundred to five hundred words.

"But, Rena...I don't know how to write an erotic short story." That's the point. You're not here to learn to become a writer; you're here to give your imagination a chance to express itself and your mind an opportunity to expand. No one else is going to read this (unless you choose to share it with them). Don't make it beautiful. Make it raw.

In the event your brain just does *not* want to cooperate, I'm giving you some intros below. These were written by Shameless clients who (like most of you) aren't professional erotic writers. If you need a place to get started, pick one of these prompts and run with it.

———

Her gown flowed behind her, revealing muscular thighs and abundant hips as she took long strides across the playa, letting her blind senses guide her. She eventually reached out and touched what seemed to be a yurt. Soft Indian music was playing within, and the smell of palo santo flooded her senses, so she opened the door flap and walked in. Before her was a beautiful man with tan skin, mid-length brown hair, and a gorgeous tattoo of a hawk on his back…

————

She applied the bright red lip stain to her lips and looked back at her reflection. *Yes*, she thought. *This is the perfect look for tonight.* In the other room, her boyfriend was waiting. They had rented the most elaborate and ornate suite the hotel had to offer. He had turned up the music, and she could feel the pulse of the beat as she prepared to enter the room…

————

Buckling the last harness of the strap-on, I was moved by a surge of masculine energy that settled smugly in my crotch. I chased away a sudden urge to mansplain crypto, and my eyes settled on the beauty before me. On the bed, she waited patiently on all fours, a plump rear presented, eager to begin…

————

It's late on a cold winter night. The best time of year: when it gets dark earlier and the wind starts to chill. We've been watching holiday movies on the couch with a fire burning in the fireplace. The air outside is still; anyone would be insane to leave the comfort of their homes. We're on the couch, wrapped up in blankets and each other. As we both relax and take in the moment, our hands begin to wander…

———

Dressed in her sassiest boot heels and sexy leather jacket, she strutted down the high street toward the local train station. It was a bright day, and the sun reflected off her brunette hair, catching the auburn highlights. Waiting on the platform, she tilted her face to the sun and enjoyed the hit of vitamin D. Suddenly she felt a large, firm hand on her pert ass, and a deep, husky voice whispered into her ear, "Hey, sexy. What's up?"

———

It's often said the biggest sex organ is the one between our ears (i.e., our brains). And if writing this story has awoken your sleeping sexual tiger, *bravissima*. You're off to a great start!

But having an appetite is only the first step. You may find that you can get into the mood…and then get sucked right out of it once you've hit the bed. How do you drown out that annoying, off-topic voice?

Start by bringing yourself back to the room and your body. And I don't mean this in some sort of metaphysical or spiritual way. I mean this quite literally.

Ever tried meditating? It's hard. Really hard at the beginning. (And for me, it hasn't really gotten much easier.) During meditation, they tell you that if your mind starts to wander, bring yourself back to your breath. Focus on each inhale and exhale. If your mind wanders a hundred times, you bring yourself back to your breath a hundred times, and you don't judge yourself for being shitty at meditation.

The same goes for sex: any time your mind wanders, focus on one part of your body where you're being touched or feeling pleasure. Just one. And if your mind starts wandering again, bring your focus back as many times as you need to.

To make that easier, give yourself other ways to engage your senses. Light a scented candle (which will give you a smell to focus on). Play some music (which will give you a sound to focus on). Create some ambient lighting, so you can actually find objects in the room to look at.

Oof. Did that last one—having the lights on—make you squirm a little?

As someone who insisted on lights off for the first ten years of being sexually active, I totally get it. I reasoned if the person I was getting naked with didn't have to look at my body, then they wouldn't be focusing on my flaws and imperfections. What the hell would they be focusing on then? I'd never really stopped to think of that.

Masters and Johnson coined the term *spectatoring*, which is a fancy way of saying that you're looking at your own body through someone else's eyes during sex. Your body is physically there, but your mind is over in the corner of the room judging you like an asshole. If you're spectatoring during sex, then—by definition—you're not actually present. Insisting on having the lights off can be a way to quiet the asshole in the corner, right? "You can't see me anymore!" But it doesn't mean the jerk has disappeared.

One client I worked with—Gina—hadn't had sex with the lights on since her kids were born. "I never lost my baby weight," she told me, "and I feel really insecure in my body." On the rare occasion she and her husband would have sex during the daytime, she held on to the covers for dear life and avoided any position where she'd be on full display.

As you know by now, the only way to start getting comfortable—and confident—is by doing the damned thing, in the babiest of steps. Gina didn't jump right into full-blown, bright-light, uncovered sex. No, she started by leaving the bathroom light on, which brightened up their adjoining bedroom just a tad. The next time, she pushed the covers to the side.

Was this scary and nerve-racking for her at the beginning? Of course. But she knew she couldn't have something different if she kept doing more of the same.

And these small (read: huge) acts of bravery had major impacts. "We're both enjoying sex so much more," she told me during our next session. They were both seen, literally and figuratively.

Does this mean that lights-off sex is always a no-no? Absolutely not. Variety is important after all! But if that's your default setting, start gently working up to showing more of yourself. Maybe it's a candle or a night-light. Maybe it's leaving the door open and hallway light on (or bathroom light, like Gina did). And then— maybe eventually—it's having sex in the daylight, the covers in a heap in the bedroom corner.

Start gently moving out of your head and into your body and enjoy that delicious meal you've been craving!

Talk about It

recently had a discussion with a grief coach about the parallels between death and sex, two topics that people avoid talking about.

Why we struggle to speak about grief makes sense: we're hard-wired to fear death. Talking about a loved one dying reminds us of our own mortality. It's uncomfortable. In short, we avoid talking about death because we don't want to die.

But sex? Sex is something most of us have done, are doing, or want to do. We're hardwired to *not* avoid it in order to keep our species alive. And yet it's the topic that makes folks squirm the most. It's considered impolite conversation. It gets censored on social media.

As a DA, I had no issues discussing it. Terms like "forced oral copulation," "digital penetration," and "sexual battery" were part of my daily vernacular. I wouldn't have been able to do my damned job as a sex crimes prosecutor if I couldn't bring myself to use words to describe every sex act imaginable. But none of these involved me. None of these involved the sheer joy of sex. Instead of talking about a meal as a chef would, I was approaching it from the perspective of a food inspector or infectious disease specialist: clinically and on the hunt for danger.

The messages you received regarding sex may be similarly clinical or apprehensive. Your religion may have taught you sex is dirty. Your family may have not talked about sex at all... or only in the context of avoiding pregnancy. Your sex education likely focused on STIs and all the ways sex can go *wrong*. If you find it hard to discuss sex as a pleasant experience, it makes complete sense. No one has given you the vocabulary to do it any other way. It's like being dropped into the streets of Mexico after taking a semester of high school Spanish: you're stumbling through it (at best) and feeling absolutely terrified (at worst).

And here's the rub: being able to talk about sex outside the bedroom boosts your overall relationship satisfaction. Research by the Gottman Institute tells us that 50 percent of women who discuss their sexual feelings with their husbands were "very satisfied" with the relationship.

And women who didn't talk about it? That number dropped down to 9 percent. *Nine percent.*

When we're looking at a range as huge as 50 percent and 9 percent, we can't treat sexual discussions as a "nice to have"—a cherry on top—in relationships. Being able to talk about sex can be what makes or breaks it.

Does this mean you have to start shouting about sex from the proverbial rooftops? No, it doesn't. Does this mean you have to be the couple who talks about kinks and threesomes while sitting inches away from other restaurant patrons? Absolutely not. (Though yes, I am that couple.) As someone who's spent her entire working life—first as a sex crimes prosecutor, now as an intimacy coach—talking about sex, it comes easily to me...now. But it took practice and a hell of a lot of discomfort to be able to talk about it personally rather than professionally.

"Oh, great. So this is going to be hard." Probably. But the good news is you don't have to reinvent the wheel here. I'm going to give you an entire tool kit of options to get you started.

Let's go.

Try Sensate Focus

Back in Lesson 8, "Turn Yourself On," I introduced you to the solo version of sensate focus. The practice was designed to get you curious about what types of sensation, pressure, and touch you like on your body and *where* you like it. But sensate focus was originally designed as a tool for couples, and it's one I love recommending to partnered folks as a way to help them gradually start using their words in the bedroom.

The practice happens over the course of four weeks and builds week by week. Talk to your partner, and figure out a time each week when you can dedicate forty uninterrupted minutes for the practice. That might look like "Wednesday after the kids go to bed" or "Sunday morning after breakfast." Get it on the calendar ASAP!

GROUND RULES

Each week, you'll start by going into the bedroom together, dimming the lights, and playing some relaxing music to set the scene. You'll each take off all your clothes (yep—fully naked!) and get on the bed.

Decide who partner A is and who partner B is. (Every week, you'll alternate who is A and who is B.) Set a timer for twenty minutes. During that time, partner A will touch partner B as described below. Once that timer goes off, set another timer for twenty minutes and switch roles (partner B will touch partner A).

The goal here isn't to give a massage! The goal is to feel pleasure and provide feedback to each other about what feels good. Use your words ("I like it when you tickle me there"), or give other auditory or nonverbal cues to let them know what you're enjoying. You can also place your hand on top of your partner's hand and guide them to indicate how you'd like to be touched.

WEEKLY RULES

- Week One: Breasts/nipples, butt, and genitals are off-limits. The rest of the body is fair game.
- Week Two: Genitals are off-limits.
- Week Three: Penetration (with a penis, finger, toy, anything) is off-limits. Orgasm is allowed.
- Week Four: Game on! Both penetration and orgasm are on the menu.

And yes, you can still have sex (however you define it) outside these sessions! These are by no means meant to limit you and how you connect. This is merely a dedicated time and space once per week to connect in a different way.

There's also a pretty good chance the session may *lead to sex*, even if it's not "supposed" to. Most of the women I've worked with have come back and reported they "failed" the earlier exercises because they ended up getting down and dirty with their partner. If that happens to you, know that you didn't fail at all! Just remember: the purpose of the exercise is for you to use your words and take turns doing so. If things start heating up right away, take a step back and remind yourselves of the task at hand. In the moment, you can even promise some sort of reward if you can keep your hands in the green zones ("If we can get through this and play by the rules, let's go for ice cream after!"). Or if those twenty minutes feel like an eternity and you need to shorten the duration to five minutes per person to keep you on track, do it.

Share Your List

Yep. It's as simple as it sounds.

You've got your list of 27 Things you want to do, be, or experience in your intimate life. Ask your partner to come up with their own list, and then share them with each other. Then take turns scratching things off your respective bucket lists. I recommend each of you pick an item off your partner's list (instead of picking something off your own list) so that you're individually in control of boundaries and pacing.

And then pick a frequency that you'll use to accomplish your picks. This might be once a week or once a month. ·

"Hey, You Know What Might Be Fun to Try?"

Every so often, I'll work with a client who doesn't want her partner to know she's hired an intimacy coach. In those situations, there's no natural way of saying "Here's a list of 27 Things I decided to come up with" without confusing the hell out of her partner. You may be similarly situated and have your own reasons for not telling your mate you've picked up this book. But you still have goals you're hoping to accomplish. Fantasies you're yearning to actualize. Positions you're eager to try. *An entire list to get through*. And you may not know where the hell to start.

"Hey, you know what might be fun to try?" is your magic bullet.

My client Carmen is originally from Venezuela and grew up in a culture where, in her words, "If you talk about what you like sexually, you're a whore."

Now married to an American man, she came to me because her sex life had become stale, which had her worried her marriage might not survive. "He doesn't know I'm working with you," she explained, "but I feel like it's my responsibility to speak up, tell him what I want. I have no idea how to do it though."

She noticed when they'd had sex recently, he'd started focusing more on her anus. Exploring with his fingers. The idea turned her on, but she couldn't get over the physical discomfort she was feeling when he'd do it. When we started working together, she confessed that she'd secretly bought a butt plug and was using it on her own when she'd masturbate as a way to "practice." It turned out *that* felt really good.

"I want to be able to bring it into the bedroom," she told me, "but I'm scared to tell him I've been using it."

I firmly believe we as humans are entitled to autonomy when we masturbate. It's no one else's business how we do it, what (if anything) we watch while doing it, or what we fantasize about while we're doing it.

"You don't have to tell him you've been using the plug," I explained to Carmen, "but you *can* suggest using it together."

How?

During our session, I asked her to pull up the Amazon listing for the same butt plug she'd been using on her own. She took a screenshot of it on her phone and texted the screenshot to her husband along with "Hey, you know what might be fun to try?" Within minutes, he responded, letting her know he was game for it. Their son would be at a sleepover that Saturday night, so she followed up with "How about we play around with it while he's at the sleepover on Saturday?" Again, he was on board.

"The sex was ten out of ten," she told me during our next session.

"What would you have ranked it at before?" I asked.

"Oh, like a two out of ten."

Week after week, she continued texting him new ideas: "What do you think about me bringing a vibrator into the bedroom on our next date? Want to pick a night this week to shop for toys online together? I heard about a thing called sensate focus. Mind if I send you an email about it?" The texts got easier week after week.

Use "Hey, you know what might be fun to try?" as your spring-board. Watch how high you'll soar!

There's an App for That!

Yes, we're all glued to our phones. Yes, technology has changed human connection as we now know it.

Despite the pitfalls that accompany our dependence on smart-phones, they can be valuable allies when it comes to opening up sexual dialogues with our partners. There's an app for everything, right? Sex is no different.

There are two apps I recommend most to partnered clients: Paired and Spicer. Both require you *each* download the app.

Paired sends you and your partner a question every day, prompting a short-form response. Most of the questions aren't sexual ("Which of your past dates would you most want to recreate?" "What would the title of your partner's biography be?"), but you'll regularly get prompts like "Using sex toys together: yes or no? Why?" or "What's your favorite sex act to receive?" or "Is it ever okay to fake an orgasm? Why or why not?" You're only able to see your partner's response once you've submitted your own. Paired is a great way for couples to connect on *all* levels and is particularly good for easing you into sexual conversations.

If you're ready to get down to business and hone in specifically on sex, try the Spicer app. Unlike Paired (which requires you to type out an answer), Spicer will send each of you a sexual prompt for the day and give you three options to respond: thumbs up (meaning yes, I would do that), thumbs down (meaning hell no), or both thumbs up and down (meaning maybe). Some examples:

- Have feet licked by partner
- Be dominated by partner during oral sex
- Go to a sex shop together

If both of you say yes or maybe to a prompt, you'll both get an alert notifying you of the match. Under each match, the app provides a dedicated thread where you can strike up a dialogue with each other about the match itself. There are other functionalities within the app too, where you can challenge each other, create wish lists, and incentivize your partner with rewards.

You can also ask the app to send you random challenges based on your matches. My partner and I have used these random challenges to give us a guidepost for our evening rendezvous, because "use food during sex" may not be something you'd think of doing on a random Tuesday night.

Paired and Spicer are two apps out of many. Have a look on your app store, and see what jumps out at you. If you don't like one, try another. The key is to be consistent about using the app daily so your conversational exploration doesn't stall. I check into my apps right after I finish my morning journaling and before checking email. If you can pair checking the app with another activity you already do daily (e.g., brushing your teeth), you're less likely to forget to do it.

Create a Dedicated Channel of Communication

Apps are great for giving you a dedicated and safe space to chat about sex, but you can easily create your own instead of (or in addition to) them. In a world where so much of our communication is transactional or logistical, Esther Perel recommends couples create a unique email address for sending love notes to one another. If you're more of a texter, try using a different texting platform with your partner, one that's dedicated solely to communicating about sex or your relationship. WhatsApp, Telegram, and Voxer are great (and free!) options.

A separate texting channel is particularly useful if you have kids, for a few reasons. One, if your text thread is typically cluttered with complaints about diaper explosions or requests to pick up food from the store, it's probably not gonna get you in the mood to talk about ripping each other's clothes off. Two, if your family shares screens (e.g., your kids borrow your iPad), you won't have to worry about them accidentally seeing anything. (I legit know someone whose kids saw sexy photos she'd sent to their dad—not the end of the world but not ideal.)

Make It a Game

There are so, so many ways to gamify your sex life. In addition to the apps I recommended above, there are apps designed for you to play in person together. Gottman Card Decks is a great starting point. Within the app, there are various card decks to pick from, ranging from "date questions" to "sex questions." In the latter deck are questions like "What can I do to help you feel aroused?" and "Is it hard for you to ask for what you want when it comes to touch?"

Have a long road trip coming up? Have the passenger bring out the app to start a dialogue. In a long-distance relationship? Take turns picking questions, screenshot them, and send them to each other.

Within the Gottman app, there's an additional set of "salsa" decks that range from mild to medium to hot. Those are structured more as sexual suggestions or challenges ("Talk to your partner during sex" and "Make love in front of a large mirror") that you can both agree to enact.

If you're looking for tangible cards, there are dozens of decks out there. My favorite decks for broader relationship conversations are made by a company called Love Lingual. Each consists of 150 cards, broken down into categories, one of which is "Intimacy." If you're looking to focus solely on sex, I recommend a fabulous deck by a company called Wonderlust. In addition to some deep conversation starters, their deck has some "action" cards thrown in too.

Whichever route you go (even if you pick a different company's card deck), I highly recommend you don't each answer the same card. Why? Because you'll be distracted, mentally formulating your own response while trying to listen to your partner telling you theirs. Instead, take turns pulling a card and asking your partner the question on the card. Keep the piles separate, and once you've gone through the entire deck, you can swap and start over, ensuring you each have a chance to answer all the questions.

Make It Part of a Relationship Check-In

For some folks, the idea of a "check-in" might feel incredibly unromantic and a little stilted. Remember that group of one hundred female attorneys I told you about in the prologue, who I presented in front of? An audience member asked how to start a dialogue with her husband about sex.

When I started talking about relationship check-ins, another audience member scoffed and said, "Who actually *does* those?"

"I do," I replied. Because I love relationship check-ins. They create a safe space to express what's on your mind: the good, the bad, and the ugly.

Many couples wait until things melt down before they start having hard conversations. They ignore the "check engine" light and don't react until the car is broken down smoking on the side of the highway. A relationship check-in is like a routine oil change: it isn't "fun," per se, but it'll help prevent unexpected breakdowns in the future.

Just like cars come with a recommended frequency for maintenance, I suggest couples have a scheduled cadence for their check-ins. Once a month works well in my relationship. I've seen couples who check in the same day every week. Pick a frequency that feels right to you, and stick with it.

Get it on the calendar, or tie it to something else you know you do regularly. Maybe the same day you water your plants or after you pay your monthly rent or mortgage.

Relationship check-ins can cover a variety of topics:

- Shared household duties
- Finances
- Childcare

But they can also involve deeper issues:

- Conflict resolution
- Overall communication

- Quality time together
- Sex

Pick the topics that are relevant to your relationship, and for each category, ask this question: "On a scale of one to ten, how do you think we managed [finances, conflict, sex, etc.] this past [week, month, etc.]?"

If the number is *lower* than ten, here's your follow-up question: "What could bring it to a ten?"

When it comes to sex, improving your score can look like any of these:

- I wish we were having more sex.
- I think it would be fun to bring toys in.
- I want to focus more on orgasm before intercourse.

This is your dedicated space to use your words. Start talking!

20

Schedule It

We have a Sunday ritual.

I show up at my partner's house. He makes us some sort of cocktail, which we sip out on the back deck. We then retreat inside where he gets started on dinner. After dinner, we return to the deck, eat a weed gummy, and play Zut.¶ After a few rounds of Zut, we stroll back inside and plop ourselves down on the living room rug. We sit across from one another crisscross applesauce, with a board game between us and a glass of whiskey within arm's reach.

And then we have mind-blowing sex that typically lasts a few hours.

"What about Monday through Saturday?" I'm often asked. For

¶ In case you're wondering what the hell I'm talking about, here's how the game works. One person picks a category (e.g., types of fabric). You each choose a noun in that category. You then go back and forth coming up with new nouns (silk, denim, cotton). If you can't think of one, you say "Zut!" and admit your defeat. We discovered this game through Amor Towles's beautiful novel *A Gentleman in Moscow*, in case you're curious!

starters, we usually spend only four nights a week together. And on those nights, sometimes we have sex. Sometimes we don't. Sometimes it's a quickie. Sometimes we bring in role-play or lean into our Dom/sub dynamic. Sometimes it's tender and vanilla.

But without fail, Sunday nights are our night. Unless one of us is traveling or there's a damned good reason for it, nothing comes between us and our weekly ritual. Sunday scaries no more. Sexy Sundays all the way.

There's a stigma around scheduling sex. Like, if you *need* to put it on a calendar, there must be something wrong with your underlying relationship. Or you're so type A that it sucks all the joy out of your intimate time together. And that couldn't be further from the truth.

My partner and I don't have kids and the accompanying bedtimes that parents have to work around. We don't have demanding work schedules that call for late-night meetings. We both live alone, so we don't have to worry about roommates hearing us.

In other words: we absolutely, positively don't *need* to schedule sex. But we do it anyway. And I'm here to tell you, regardless of what your relationship, living situation, or family dynamics look like, scheduled sex can be some of the hottest sex you'll ever have.

Don't believe me? Think of other ways you plan joy, indulgence, and connection in your life: A dinner reservation at your favorite restaurant. A milestone birthday party. A relaxing vacation.

Does the fact that you planned those events make them any less enjoyable? Of course not. In fact, you probably enjoy them *more* because of anticipation. You anticipate the delicious meal.

You anticipate the connection you'll feel at the party. You anticipate the bliss you'll experience on vacation.

Sex is no different. In fact, anticipation is even more important when it comes to sex. Here's why. Only 15 percent of women have spontaneous sexual desire. Yep, only about one in every six women wants sex out of the blue. And if you're not in that 15 percent? Instead of throwing your hands up in the air in frustration because you're not in the mood, ask yourself, "What could *get* me in the mood?"

I like to think of desire like having a sweet tooth: some of us might—out of nowhere—crave a cookie. That's spontaneous desire. For the rest of us who don't have a sweet tooth, we may crave cookies when we smell them baking in an oven or see someone eating one on TV. That's responsive desire. Think of scheduled sex as the equivalent of reading five-star Yelp reviews about the new cookie shop in town, knowing you're going to make a stop there later.**

When sex is definitively placed on your calendar, you have an incentive to get yourself in the right headspace for it. You're motivated to replicate the smell of cookies baking in the oven, sexually speaking. If you know that porn helps, watch some beforehand. If putting on some lingerie makes you feel sexy, pull some out of the drawer. What you water will grow.

I like the carrot of sex being dangled in front of me beforehand, and my partner knows this. He'll often text me on Sunday

---

** "But, Rena! My sex life isn't the equivalent of the five-star cookie shop. It's more like the sad 7-Eleven chocolate chip cookie sitting in a basket near the register." If that's the case, go back to Lesson 18 as a reminder that you'll only crave what's worth craving, and then reread Lesson 19 for tips on how to communicate what your version of a five-star cookie tastes like.

afternoon with some tiny hint as to what's to come later or request that I wear a certain item of clothing (a short skirt, black lingerie, knee-high socks, etc.). Knowing he's already thinking about our evening together is a huge fucking turn-on. But when he doesn't send those messages? I'll still do what I do to get myself mentally prepared. I'll pick out something to wear that I feel great in. I may masturbate early in the day, thinking about what's to come (pun intended) later. Or I'll get myself close to the point of orgasm, then deliberately stop.

In *Come as You Are* (a book I consider to be the bible in terms of female sexuality), Dr. Emily Nagoski discusses the concept of accelerators and brakes. Accelerators are the things that get us in the mood; brakes are the things that take us out of the mood. Each woman's accelerators and brakes are completely unique to them, though, and one woman's accelerators can be another's brakes. When I was in law school, for example, I had a friend whose libido would skyrocket during final exam season. She was insatiable, scheduling booty calls with whomever she was dating at the time (or finding someone who would get the job done). Me? The thought of sex was about as appealing as getting a root canal. For my friend, stress was pedal to the metal; for me, stress was a pile of bricks pushing down on my brakes.

Understanding there isn't a one-size-fits-all approach to accelerators and brakes, Dr. Nagoski came up with a technique to figure out what your ideal sexy contexts are. I assign this exercise as homework to my clients and will urge you to complete it yourself right now.

"Think of a positive sexual experience from your past," she instructs, "then describe it...with as many relevant details as you

can recall." Here are a few positive sexual experiences from past
Shameless clients:

———————

Bathroom sex with my ex in my family's vacation home.
Everyone was home and we snuck away. The fact that we
had to be as quiet as possible to not get caught made it
even sexier. He was forceful and passionate and caring all
at the same time. It wasn't just about his pleasure but mine
and that was his focus.

———————

It was when my husband and I first moved in together. One
night, we were watching movies and started kissing and
touching, and it led to sex. We had sex several times that
night that was carefree and fun and like time was limitless.

———————

When my wife and I had a threesome with a guy friend. He
was talking shit so my wife and I went in the next room and
locked him out. We both decided not to be shy and just enjoy
the moment. I started to feel really confident, and I could tell
she was enjoying what I was doing. Soon he made his way
into the room (fussing that we started without him) but quickly
joined in. We were so in sync and things just started happening quickly. I felt really in control as I was the one choosing
who I wanted to be with and what I wanted to do to them.

———————

When I studied abroad in Mexico, I had a relationship with a guy from my cohort. We both had host families so we could not have sex at our respective homes, but there was a stairwell and rooftop in the apartment building where I was staying, and almost every night after we went out as a group, he'd walk me home, and while we were tipsy and/or high, we would have what felt like really exciting sex in that stairwell. Once or twice, we got a room, but mostly it was that stairwell!

————

My first BDSM experience with my partner where we had planned to be sexually intimate that evening and on a whim chose to select some BDSM toys to try out together. We first talked about what we wanted to do and what it would take to make each other feel comfortable in the moment before embarking on a consensual and very liberating sexual inter-course that used blindfolds, a feather, and our new vibrator.

————

Now, "think of a not-so-great sexual experience from your past—not necessarily a terrible one, just a not-so-great one." Describe that experience. Again, here are what some of the Shameless women had to say:

————

Went home with someone after a night out. I knew it wasn't going to be more than one night. That part didn't bother me, but it was just lackluster. I felt like I wasted a night with a guy when I could have just gotten good sleep at home on my own. We had both been drinking, the sex was fine but was too fast, I didn't finish, and he didn't really care about what I needed.

———————

My partner initiated sex the other night and spent some time touching me and fingering me before penetration. I was a little tired and felt like I just couldn't get fully into the experience. I was constantly thinking and anticipating every move and whether it felt pleasurable or not so that it felt like I just could not get out of my head.

———————

I met a girl recently after putting an ad out for friends. I find her mentally engaging, but I am not physically attracted to her. At this moment, I am still sorting out if I'm attracted to "crazy" and don't know what it's like to date someone who is nice and treats me well. Or if I am just truly not attracted to her?

———————

Sex with T for the first time, after a major breakup with someone else. It was disappointing. One position, no oral, no talking. He was just heavy breathing, on top, crushing me. Duration was short. He thought it was a very good time. I felt awkward and left almost immediately afterward. He didn't offer for me to stay the night or help getting home. I left feeling very gross.

———

Last time I had sex with the father of my kids, I was six weeks postpartum. He didn't make me feel desired. He laid me back and stuck his dick in and steadily picked up pace until it hurt so bad from his grinding, I told him to stop, and he jumped off in disgust and walked away.

———

Once you've written out both your positive and not-so-great sexual experiences, Nagoski urges you to break each of them into beats, honing in on the aspects of the experience that made it positive or not so great. To make it easier, she created the following categories as prompts to use for both types of experiences:

MENTAL AND PHYSICAL WELL-BEING

- Physical health
- Body image
- Mood
- Anxiety
- Distractibility
- Worry about sexual functioning
- Other

PARTNER CHARACTERISTICS

- Physical appearance
- Physical health
- Smell

- Mental state
- Other

RELATIONSHIP CHARACTERISTICS

- Trust
- Power dynamic
- Emotional connection
- Feeling desired
- Frequency of sex

SETTING

- Private/public (at home, work, vacation, etc.)
- Distance sex (phone, chat, etc.)
- See partner do something positive, like interact with family or do work

OTHER LIFE CIRCUMSTANCES

- Work-related stress
- Family-related stress
- Holiday, anniversary, "occasion"

THINGS YOU DO

- Self-guided fantasy
- Partner-guided fantasy ("talking dirty")
- Body parts that were touched or not

- Oral sex on you/on partner
- Intercourse, etc.

After completing that exercise, you'll have a clear idea of what works for you...and what doesn't. Equipped with your unique tool kit of accelerators and brakes, you can start engineering your next sexual experience. But start by getting it on the calendar. This doesn't need to literally be on a Google shared calendar a week in advance (though it can be). As you'll see, you can literally text your partner about what you want to do together later that night.

My client Bella hadn't had sex with her husband in a year. She'd had her hands full after a rough pregnancy with twins and assumed her constant state of fatigue was the culprit for her failing libido. "When was the last time you had *great* sex with him?" I asked.

It turned out it'd been over a decade ago, before they moved in together. They'd done it plenty of times in the intervening years, but nothing she qualified as "great."

"He's super respectful of me," she explained. "Like, he'll roll over in bed and ask me if I want to do it and I'll say yes because it's been a while. But I'm not *excited* about it." Life was pushing down on her brakes, but nothing was pushing down on her accelerator.

"You can't enjoy sex if you view it as a chore," I told her and followed up with "What's the kind you *crave*?"

She explained that she wanted him to just *take her*. Not ask permission. Not be polite about it. She also understood this was completely unrealistic based on their current relationship dynamic.

"Who puts your kids to bed?" I asked during our midafternoon session.

"Normally I do, or we do it together."

"How about you send him a text—right now—asking him to put the kids to bed tonight and tell him you'll be waiting for him in the bedroom once he's done. And then tell him you want him to 'take' you."

She winced, unsure this would work.

"Well, if it doesn't, then you're no worse off than where you started, right?" I dared her.

She reluctantly sent the text to her husband, who was working under the same roof, in a different room of the house.

Once it was the kids' bedtime, they gave each other a silent acknowledgment. He took the kids to their room, and she retreated into theirs. She put on lingerie. Lingerie with the tags still on, purchased years beforehand while in an optimistic state of mind about their sex life. She left the door open a crack, less than optimistic about what would happen when it came time for him to walk in.

Her "respectful" husband ravaged her in a way she never could have expected. There was a caged tiger inside him, and her text had been the key to set it free. "It was the best sex we've ever had."

A few weeks later, she (half-jokingly) told me I'd done my job a bit too well. "He's chasing me around all the time now. Sending me texts throughout the day, telling me all the things he's going to do to me later." Scheduling sex—hot, voracious sex—had pressed a hard reset button in their intimate lives.

But what if you struggle to find time *on* your calendar to schedule sex?

My client Josefina lamented that she and her husband were trying (and failing) at scheduling sex at night. "We're exhausted after we put our daughter to bed. The only thing I want to do is scroll Instagram and maybe cuddle with him on the couch."

"Is there a time of day you two are home alone?" I asked.

It turned out that there was about an hour window every weekday morning after they'd dropped their daughter off at school where they had the house to themselves. And they started using it to their advantage, capitalizing on having free rein of the home (hello, kitchen blow jobs!) and a full reservoir of energy.

Sex can be an escape from your to-do list. Instead of treating it like grocery shopping, view it as a nice meal out at a restaurant. Make a reservation. Show up. Feast away.

21

Make Porn Your Friend

et me tell you about the first time I sent porn to my partner.
As with most ethically produced BDSM porn, the actors in the video I'd uncovered had a conversation out of character before the scene started. They talked about boundaries, safe words, and what they were excited to enact. Lots of smiling and giggling and lightheartedness and not at all an indication of what was to come next: The woman in a locker room. The male intruder who tied a burlap sack over her head with rope and then used the rope to restrain her. He hurt her, beat her, and used every orifice in her body.

"I like the idea of this, but I'm not into the pain part," I followed up in a text to my partner, along with a link to the video. This was early in our relationship—and early into my kink journey. I didn't know how to articulate what it is I wanted, so I showed instead of told.

A few months later, we had our first weekend away together. He'd found a place that had been featured in *Vogue*—a rustic, dreamy cabin in the Ojai hills. I only later realized why he'd picked it. Why having sturdy wooden beams in the sun-drenched bedroom would be a priority.

He hadn't seen me without makeup yet. Sure, he'd seen me in the morning, but not in an exposed state, out of the shower, hair in a towel, applying my expensive skin tonics and powdering in my eyebrows. He had no idea how much care I put into making myself ready for him. And I wasn't ready for him to find out. So I took my time in the bathroom. I didn't emerge until about forty-five minutes later, fully dressed, hair dried, makeup done. I crept down the stairs toward the bedroom, ready for him to kiss me and take me into town to taste olive oil.

Instead, he ran out from the walk-in closet, grabbed me, and put a pillowcase over my head.

He'd taken great care to find one with sheer enough fabric so I wouldn't feel too claustrophobic. He'd sourced some extra long and sturdy zip ties so that he could imprison me quickly. He'd bought special medical scissors to make sure he could liberate me just as quickly if I used our safe word.

I fought. He was stronger. Strong enough to tie my wrists to the ropes he'd hung from the beams. We fucked until I sweated off all the makeup I'd carefully applied.

"Was that what you had in mind?" he asked, our sticky bodies wrapped around each other in the king-size bed.

"That's exactly what I had in mind." I was smiling, giggling, lighthearted.

And we did taste olive oil that day. We also hiked, nearly falling into an overflowing ravine. Back at the cabin, he flicked me with some water from the kitchen sink just so he could say, "Let's get you out of those wet clothes."

I didn't utter the word then, but that was the day I fell in love with him. And porn has remained one of the many ways I've shown him how to love me.

It's been said that "Watching porn to learn how to have sex is like watching NASCAR to learn how to drive." I've heard variations of this quote from so many sex educators at this point, I'm not sure who the original source is. It's clever, sure. But I think it misses the mark a bit.

No, porn isn't a substitute for comprehensive sex ed. But it can be an incredibly powerful teacher nonetheless. Sure, I've learned a ton about BDSM and kink from watching it. But porn also taught me how to use a strap-on and that I could use the reverse cowgirl position to ride dick (a godsend for my tight hamstrings). I would've been utterly baffled the first time I made a woman squirt if I hadn't already seen it in porn.

Think I would've been exposed to any of this in sex ed? Highly unlikely.

As you saw in Lesson 2, porn caused me a ton of harm as a kid. I had unhealthy views about my body. About how to get boys to like me. About how women orgasm. I learned a lot about sex but nothing about intimacy.

You've probably heard the horror stories. Of teenagers who now expect anal on the first date because of porn. Of your friend's husband who has a porn addiction. Of the women who are exploited in the porn industry. There are entire books written about the perils of porn.

But saying "porn is evil" is like saying knives are evil because people get stabbed with them.

I'm here to champion porn as a tool. To show you the beautiful creations that can be made with the blade of this particular knife. To encourage you to tune out the fearmongering and make porn your friend.

When you think of porn, images of highly produced scenes with massive penises and gravity-defying huge breasts may come to mind. You may see porn as another world where women orgasm through a few thrusts of a penis and no one seems to need lube. You may question whether the actors (particularly the female ones) want to be there and whether they're being paid fairly. And if those are the only associations you have with porn, it makes complete sense why the idea of watching it may not appeal to you.

But there's also an entire universe of what's known as "ethical porn." Within that universe are sites dedicated to promoting fair wages, being inclusive (in terms of gender and sexual expression, age, ability, race, etc.), and even including real couples (i.e., non-actors) having sex on camera. If we see porn as a knife—a tool—think of ethical porn as the biggest butcher block imaginable, complete with a variety of blades for every conceivable task.

Want to see people who look like *you* having sex? Ethical porn can be a great normalizer. Say you're a young adult questioning your gender identity...who happens to live in a homogeneous and conservative small town. Chances are you're not seeing people who represent *you* when you go to the grocery store. A mindful search for ethical porn can be a way to "find your people" in the sense that it shows you there are people like you *out there*, enjoying themselves sexually.

Or you may be a heterosexual cisgender woman who feels like she's "not sexy" because she doesn't conform to conventional beauty standards. Search for ethical porn with nonactors. I assure you, they're more representative of what naked bodies *actually* look like than any half-naked models on Instagram.

My client Leah—who'd never watched porn in her entire life—saw the value in it, but she had to get over a few initial reservations first. After I assured her she wouldn't get a virus on her computer, she picked a night when her kids would be with their dad. Once she had the house to herself, she turned off all the lights in her bedroom, closed the curtains, and hid under the covers with her laptop. (Not necessary, but it helped ease her mind.)

I suggested she watch as many clips as possible, a few minutes at a time. "Aim for thirty minutes total, if you can."

She ended up watching three hours' worth.

"I couldn't believe all the shapes and sizes," she said during our next session. And she wasn't referring to penises. Porn had created a dent in dismantling a lifetime's worth of indoctrination about what naked women look like, specifically who is "allowed" to be sexual...and sexy.

So where do you begin? Bellesa is the site I recommend most as a starting point. Why? Because they place female pleasure at the center of their films. I'll quote from their own mission statement here:

Bellesa Films captures real, unscripted sex. No fake orgasms, ever. Performers are encouraged to communicate with their partner(s) throughout about what feels good/what they like... All Bellesa Films features begin with a fantasy, usually based on a suggestion from one of Bellesa's community members. The Bellesa team sources a powerful female performer—who then details which other performer she would most like to work with, what "kind" of sex she wants to have for this shoot and her "dos and don'ts." She is the protagonist of the scene—and her genuine pleasure is at the forefront. A script is then written to match the chosen fantasy and type of sex.

Once on the Bellesa site, you can choose from a wide variety of genres (rough, anal, girl on girl, sensual, etc.). Bellesa offers a ton of free content and an additional extended library for paid memberships.

The majority of their films are scripted, as described above. Which may not be your cup of tea. Some women thrive on a plot line, and some are taken right out of the mood by it. While Bellesa does feature a "homemade" section of their library, it's limited compared to the other genres on offer.

If you crave homemade, MakeLoveNotPorn is a great option. Here's their jam:

#realworld people—singles, couples, moresomes—capturing their #RealWorldSex the way it actually happens in their everyday lives. It's the folks from all walks of life—people just like you sharing their love… We want to see how you actually have sex in the real world. In all its crazystupidfunnysexystupendousmessysillydownanddirtylovingcasualhumanness. We don't want to see you making porn like they do in porn world. Every video…has been hand-selected by the MLNP Curatorial Team to ensure our videos are consensual, contextualized, and porn-cliche free.

The platform is subscription based and operates on a revenue-sharing model with the #realworld people who contribute their videos.

Lustery is another great site with its own monthly membership model. The company describes itself as "a creator-centered platform focused on providing a sex-celebrating and shame-free space for couples to share their love and lust with the world."

If you're searching specifically for queer ethically produced porn, CrashPadSeries is a fantastic option. They've created a space where "LGBTQ+ adult film performers can share their sexuality in an environment that is inclusive, professional, and fun and dedicated to producing sexy and exciting images that reflect today's blurred gender lines and fluid sexualities."

If you're looking for ethical BDSM porn, Kink.com has you covered: "BDSM is about respect and trust. When you watch a Kink.com movie, you are watching real BDSM-loving people play in this context. We at Kink.com pride ourselves in the authentic reproduction of fetish activities enjoyed by those in the BDSM lifestyle."

This is by no means an exhaustive list of ethical porn options (and might be even less exhaustive by the time you read this book). A quick Google search for "ethical porn sites" will yield a slew of articles that send you further down the rabbit hole if that's what you're looking for!

Also, if you've tried the above and found it's done nothing for you, fear not! Some people are more auditory than visual. If you'd rather hear your porn than watch it, consider audio erotica. Dipsea has become the household name for sexy narratives: "We are as obsessive about our characters' consent and chemistry as we are about building a culture where all perspectives and preferences are welcome." Ethical *and* steamy!

Now that we have some options to get you started, though, let's talk about how to *use* porn. (It's a tool, after all.)

First, porn is your friend when you masturbate. One study found that women who watch it during self-pleasure get aroused more quickly and orgasm more reliably (and reported more pleasure with the orgasms too!).

"Wait, does this mean partnered sex won't be as good without it then?"

Great question, and the answer is no. The same study found that porn consumption during masturbation didn't deteriorate sexual functioning during partnered sex. Win-win.

Porn can also help you explore what turns you on. If you're early on your sexual discovery journey, get curious. Watch as many different types of porn as possible, and ask yourself: What turns me on? What doesn't turn me on? Is this something that I'd actually want to do IRL?

That last question is important. Not every fantasy (i.e., the thing that turns you on sexually) is a wish (i.e., something you want to enact). I enjoy watching cisgender, male-on-male porn. Seeing penises arouses me. I'm a cisgendered woman who is (fairly) certain in her gender identity. In other words, there's no way I could actually enact strictly male-on-male porn, but it turns me the hell on.

In this vein, I get asked often by self-identifying straight women what the deal is with enjoying "lesbian" porn. (I put that in quotes because oftentimes the women featured in mainstream female-on-female porn aren't lesbians.)

"Does that mean I'm bisexual?" is the most common question.

The answer is, again, no. Or at least not necessarily. A 2018 study by Pornhub showed that lesbian porn was "by far" the most popular porn category viewed by women (and significantly more popular with women than with men). Lesbian porn—by definition—focuses solely on female pleasure, which may explain why it's a go-to for women, even those who have no real-world desire to sleep with women.

If what we watch in porn were a direct reflection of our sexual wishes, a lot of us would be banging the AC repair man or having threesomes with our babysitters. So instead of going into an existential spiral about your fantasies, ask yourself: What is it about this type of porn that turns me on? Is it the penises? Is it the focus on female pleasure? Is it the power differential? Or is it simply that it's taboo? The *why* behind the fantasy is normally a lot less scary than what's actually in the fantasy.

Say you come across a type of porn that you *want* to enact though. *Use it as a way to communicate.* I started this lesson with a story about the kinky porn I'd sent my partner. You'll remember I passed it along as a blueprint but made clear that there were parts of it (the pain, mainly) that didn't appeal to me. Start a similar dialogue with your partner.

This can look like "Hey, you know what might be fun to try? How about we each find some porn we like and send it to each other?"

Make it crystal clear that you're each coming from a place of curiosity rather than judgment. A solid follow-up question like "What is it about this that turns you on?" works wonders.

This blueprint approach is also ideal for folks who approach sex differently. I once worked with a woman whose partner is on the autism spectrum. She craved more spontaneity, and he wanted clear direction. She found some porn that intrigued her and sent that to him as inspiration. Both boxes checked.

"Okay. So does that mean we have to watch it together?" you might be wondering.

That's entirely up to you. I've been there and done that and have found it takes me out of the mood. I have no idea where to look and end up distracted as a result, eyes darting from my partner back to the screen back to my partner. It's like the sexual version of not knowing what to do with my hands. I don't love it.

For some couples, watching porn together can be incredibly helpful. If you're considering a threesome, for example, seeing your partner get turned on while people fuck on the screen can be a nice way to gauge your jealousy response.

It can also bridge a sexual orientation gap. I had a client whose husband had recently come out as bisexual, much to her surprise. Despite his assurances, she struggled to believe he was still attracted to her. I suggested they find some porn depicting group sex with both men and women swapping in every configuration imaginable.

"Men can enjoy being with men *and* women. Women can enjoy being with men *and* women" was the lesson she learned.

Porn can also present a way to discover new bedroom accessories. My client Charity knew she wanted to explore bondage but had no clue what *type* of bondage. Was it ropes? Cuffs? Shackles? By delving into the world of BDSM porn, she was able to get specific: "I realized I'm attracted to metal implements and *really* want to try an anal hook!" I've had many clients come back to me after their porn deep dive asking me about toys they've seen. Porn provides a way to watch the toys used in real time (an option not typically available on toy retailers' websites).

When you make porn your friend—as a learning tool, as a mode of communication, or as a visual that brings you pleasure during *self*-pleasure!—you step away from judgment and toward curiosity.

22

Bring in the Toys

When I tell women—the women I educate on the very topic of faking orgasms, many of whom admit to faking on a regular basis—that I've only ever done it once, they construe it as a badge of honor. They assume I must be so sexually empowered—so sure in my voice and dedicated to my pleasure—that I've reached some level of enlightenment.

The truth is I just went without orgasms during sex. Sometimes for years at a time. And there is nothing honorable about that.

As is true of many women, I take prescription medication for my mental health. I've experienced sexual side effects from them, the most noticeable being that I need a vibrator in order to orgasm. Vaginal penetration alone never did the trick (as it doesn't for roughly 85 percent of women). Oral sex used to be a reliable path for me, but that all changed when I started taking the medication I needed to keep me sane.

In short, if I'm going to come, I need some motorized support in the bedroom. And not everyone is okay with that.

The first guy I dated after going on my meds broke up with me because we weren't sexually compatible. "I just don't feel like we're having 'actual sex' if I'm not making you come."

A short while later, I got into a serious relationship with someone who didn't seem to mind having the toys around. About six months in—months where he'd spent holidays with my family, told me he loved me, and suggested we move in together—his tune changed. We were in bed one night, rolling around naked. I reached into my nightstand (as usual) to retrieve my buzzing friend.

Before he could even see it, he said, "How about we leave the vibrator out this time?" I didn't put up a fight that night. Maybe he just wanted some variety?

The days without the toy passed. Those days became months. Those months became years. And those years became half a decade.

And in those five years, we did move in together. We got married. We sent out Christmas cards.

He never brought it up again. Neither did I. Why? Because this was yet another reminder of the fact that I was forever changed by my mental health—which was not to be spoken of in casual conversation. It was yet another way in which I was different. And I so desperately wanted to be perceived as "normal."

My pleasure became my secret. One relegated to solo quickies while my husband was gone for a few hours running errands or out of town on business. Was that fucked up? Sure it was.

One night, in the throes of a whiskey-soaked argument, I

finally said something: "How am I supposed to feel about our sex life when you don't care about my pleasure?"

"You're the only woman I've ever met who can't come the normal way."

The "normal way."

I wanted to crawl into a cave and cry-scream into the void.

"Either a lot of those women were lying to you, or you'd better go out and buy a fucking lottery ticket, because you happen to be the luckiest man on earth," I countered.

But did I leave? Not then I didn't. I just felt more broken. The broken woman whose husband stayed with her. The broken woman who came from a "tacky, gauche family" vis-à-vis his WASPy, sexually repressed one.

I wondered: Was this such a huge price to pay for the stability this marriage afforded me? Was the fact that I'd only orgasmed solo for the last five-plus years enough to warrant leaving? *Would anyone else want a broken woman anyway?*

It was through my inner healing that I realized I wasn't broken, I was just different. And it's okay to be different. In fact, *it's better to be different*. The world would be pretty boring if we were all the same, wouldn't it?

I didn't know then what I know now. Sure, I knew from chats with friends that there were a hell of a lot of women out there who couldn't orgasm "the normal way," but I didn't fully appreciate how the female body functions and why only about one in five women can orgasm reliably from penetration alone. The lawyer in me knew how to argue, but I didn't have the evidence to support my case.

But more importantly, I didn't understand that pleasure is

my birthright. That I was missing out on one of life's greatest joys that is absolutely free. You have to know there's injustice occurring in order to truly fight for it.

Now that I'm a coach, my fighting spirit comes out when I work with women who are insecure about how they climax.

"How do you reach orgasm, alone or with a partner?" is a question every client answers on her intake form.

One client, Hope, responded with "I think of a story of passion where someone really desires me and I play music that makes me feel sensual and use a vibrator usually over my clothes. Have not come with a partner. Have faked many with my last partner."

She'd left a lengthy, abusive (both emotionally and sexually) relationship and had finally entered back onto the dating scene. By the time we started working together, she was a few months into a relationship with a fantastic guy. They'd taken the physical part of the relationship slowly.

"We just recently started having sex, and I shut down every time it happens. I freeze up. I cry. I tell him to stop. And he does. He's so considerate. But I know he won't be patient forever. And will this go on forever?"

"No. It won't go on forever," I told her. "Your brain and body are literally going into a trauma response now when you have sex. They're doing that to protect you. Think about it: for years, sex was abuse to you. Why would your body allow you to remain in a state that it sees as dangerous?"

Within a matter of weeks, we got her to a point where she was no longer in a trauma response during sex with her new partner.

But pleasure isn't just the lack of pain. "So how *is* the sex?" I asked.

"The sex is good! I mean, I'm not having orgasms or anything, but he doesn't know that."

I saw we still had some ways to go. Unlike a small minority of my clients, she'd had orgasms before, but never with a partner. She only used her vibrator in private. So I asked the obvious question:

"Have you ever brought the toy into the bedroom with you?"

"I don't want to make anyone feel bad about themselves, you know?" Hope admitted.

Yes, I do know.

"So none of these guys ever asked what they could do differently to make you come?"

"No, because I always faked it. They thought they were making me come."

At which point I launched into a diatribe, giving her the words I wished someone had given me when I was in an orgasm-less marriage:

"So here's the thing. Only about 15 percent of women can orgasm just through penetration. You can't train your body to orgasm that way. It's literally that their external clitorises are under 2.5 centimeters away from their vaginal opening. So they're still getting the external stimulation they need while they're being penetrated.

"And some women need more than that anyway. I'm one of them. I need a vibrator to come. A finger won't do it. Oral sex used to, but not anymore because of the medication I'm on. This is the way my body is built, and there's nothing wrong with it.

"If this guy is as great as he sounds, he will completely understand that you need something more than just penetration to make you orgasm. And from what you've told me, he really wants you to feel good. So tell him how to do it."

And that was when the alarm bells rang for her. She knew what I was going to say next.

"Oh god. You're going to tell me that I have to tell him I've been faking it, aren't you?" Her head dropped to her hands. I could see through my Zoom screen she was more distraught than she'd been at any point in the four weeks we'd already spent working together.

"Well, I'll level with you. By faking orgasms, you're training someone to do exactly what doesn't work for you. Right now, you're pretty early on in your relationship. You've been honest with him about your sexual trauma, and he's been patient and caring while you've worked through that. I think he will totally understand if you tell him that you've been dishonest, *why* you've been dishonest, and that you want to do this relationship right."

"But I have to tell him *now*?"

"If you do it now, he'll understand. The longer you wait, though, the bigger the deception becomes. Can you imagine how he'll feel a year from now if you tell him he hasn't been pleasing you at all and you've been lying about it?"

She let out a big, resigned sigh. "I'll tell him tonight." I asked her to report back to me and let me know how the conversation went.

I received the following message from her the next day: "Well, he didn't break up with me and he wasn't even upset with me... I was pretty mortified to do it but I told him everything regardless. Now he wants to meet my vibrator. Haha. I am super proud of myself and feeling excited for what is to come. He seemed surprised of course that I hadn't actually orgasmed and also that I couldn't do it with my fingers either... I just told him that's what my body needs, a vibrator...and just can't climax any other way at this point."

Bravo, woman. Bra-fucking-vo.

I'm proud to say not only has Hope's partner met her vibrator (and she's having lots of orgasms!), but they've gone toy shopping together too. Over a year later and they're still in a loving, healthy, and sexy relationship.

Does that conversation seem scary? Are you worried about making your partner feel inadequate at the mere suggestion of using toys? You're not alone. So let me offer you a reframe: Think of it like suggesting a new recipe. Or a weekend getaway. Or a hot restaurant everyone's been talking about. This doesn't need to be a serious "We need to talk about how you're not satisfying me in the bedroom" conversation. Instead, use the question you know so well by now: "Hey, you know what might be fun to try?" And go from there. Remember: this is something new you are trying together. It's a collaboration, not a competition.

If you're nervous about incorporating toys in the bedroom (or your partner has already signaled they don't want to be "replaced" by them), buy something together. This doesn't have to be at a brick-and-mortar store either. There's no shortage now of online sex toy retailers with a vast range of price points. You can either shop online together or send each other links to a few toys that pique your interests and pick one (or more!) from there. When it arrives, start by letting your partner use the toy on you. Instead of feeling like the toy is replacing them, they will see that the toy is part of them. It's just another tool they can use to bring pleasure to you.

So what kind of toy? Start with a vibrating wand. The bigger, the better. The Hitachi Magic Wand is the most well-known toy in this category. It's huge, powerful, and seen as the household name when it comes to large vibrating wands. I don't personally love it because I find the texture of the head to be a bit rough (which, combined with the wand's sheer horsepower, can lead to chafing!). There are plenty of similar models made by woman-owned toy companies that deliver the same power but with a smooth silicone finish.

"But I use a small bullet vibrator when I do things on my own."

Yes, you probably do. But here's the thing: when you use something small, you need to use it with a ton of precision. One centimeter in the wrong direction can be the difference between having an orgasm and not feeling any stimulation at all." And while *you* probably know where that one centimeter is, your partner likely doesn't.

A vibrating wand has a large head, which in turn provides plenty of surface area for your partner to work with, meaning precision isn't as important, which is a great place to start! And just as importantly, it is powerful. Like, extremely powerful. If partnered orgasm is the goal, this is the single most efficient and effective way to reach it.

Once you're both comfortable with having a wand in the bedroom, then you can discuss bringing in something smaller that you can hold in your hand and use on yourself in whatever positions you like most. (Or you can both take turns using the wand.) You can also start talking about other toys if they turn you on.

The key is to set you and your partner up for success. The toy isn't just *your* friend, *it's their friend too*.

Here are a few ways Shameless clients have incorporated toys into their sex lives:

- Chantal and her husband of thirteen years had "no spice" in the bedroom. She was insecure about receiving oral sex, and missionary position was their default setting. They ordered a vibrating wand (their first sex toy!), and it did wonders.

"He's used the wand during oral and when we're in different positions. We tried doggy style the other night too!"

- Tay underwent a long period of drug and alcohol addiction in her early adulthood. During that time, she also masturbated "compulsively." Once she got sober, she gave up self-pleasure too. "I'm worried that correlation is too strong. It's been a decade since I've masturbated." She ordered a new vibrator and inaugurated it by setting a scene that looked nothing like her addiction days. She gave herself a pedicure. She created some ambient lighting. *She broke the association.* "I've finally found a nondestructive way to surrender control."

- Emilie is in her fifties, and orgasms had become elusive. "As I get older, it's harder for me to have them on my own." She'd started seeing someone new and introduced a rabbit vibrator into the mix. "It was the first time in fifteen years I orgasmed with a partner!"

- Monique had no issues reaching orgasms on her own but clammed up around her partner. "I have a hard time feeling safe and giving up control." She got a new vibrating wand and started using it privately. Then she used it with him lying next to her. She gradually let him have his hand on hers as she maneuvered the toy. Once she was able to reach orgasm that way, it was a smooth transition into passing control of the wand over to him. Voilà!

While sex toys can be tools for orgasm, above all, they're *toys*. Have fun with them!

23

Use Your Imagination

"Would the passenger in seat 1A please report to the cockpit?"

That was me, I realized. Smoothing my short dress, I stood up and shuffled forward.

"Ma'am, I'm the pilot on this plane," the man in the white shirt and tie explained. "We have a new form of technology we're testing out, and we need your help to do it."

He gestured down toward a chair, a large dildo attached to it, and as I realized how exactly I'd need to operate this "plane," I burst into laughter.

"This is fucking ridiculous. And wait, is that a boat captain's hat you're wearing?"

My partner takes direction well, and on this particular night, the direction had come from a card game I'd bought called Caught in the Act. The card we'd picked suggested he act as the pilot and invite a sexy passenger into the cockpit. The "technology" part he'd cleverly improvised.

When it comes to role-play, you might be thinking of scenes like this. Orchestrated. Costumed. A true test of one's shitty acting skills.

And that might be your thing. When I told this story to a friend at a pool party a year later, her eyes lit up. "That's so fucking hot" were her words.

"Not to me," I said. It was absurd, a story I recount as a way to show that sex is meant to be fun, one of the few ways we—as adults—get to play.

As kids, we pretended to be princesses or bakers. We relished the delight of assuming different identities. We escaped into imaginary worlds where we lost track of time. Worlds where there was no winner or loser. Worlds where the journey was paramount and we had no destination.

Sexual fantasies provide us with a way to reclaim that childlike wonder. To remember who we were before we had to worry about 401(k)s Pap smears. To remind us how to play.

Having now experimented with various types of role-play, I know what doesn't work for me (e.g., pilot/passenger play) and what does (e.g., having a bag tied around my head by an "intruder").

If the idea of a carefully orchestrated scene appeals to you, you now have plenty of tools to start working with. Porn. The erotic short story you wrote earlier. Apps like Spicer. Hell, you can even pick up the card deck I mentioned above. Use those as a way to talk about it with your current or prospective partner.

But say all the costumes and props make your eyes roll. Does this mean you *don't* have fantasies? Absolutely not. As you'll soon find out, most of our sexual fantasies don't involve any role-play at all.

And they're super fucking important. Don't believe me? Believe the people who are way smarter than me. According to Esther Perel, "sexual fantasies reveal our deepest emotional needs." Research by Justin J. Lehmiller of the Kinsey Institute also tells us couples who share their sexual fantasies reported having the happiest relationships. The. Happiest. Relationships.

Lehmiller wrote an entire book (which I can't recommend enough) on the topic. If you're interested in diving deep on the science of sexual fantasies, *Tell Me What You Want* is the place to do it. Lehmiller took on the monumental task of creating the most comprehensive survey *ever* on the topic after realizing that when it comes to sex, there was a ton of research on what people were *doing* but very little on what people were *thinking* about.

I'm not going to write a whole book report here, but I do want to give you some key takeaways. First, "A sexual fantasy is any mental picture that comes to mind while you're awake and ultimately turns you on." *Any* mental picture, friends. Thinking of what your barista looks like naked? Sexual fantasy. Getting excited about having sex with your Tinder hookup for the first time? Sexual fantasy. Imagining being the center of a gang bang while you masturbate? Sexual fantasy. No role-play necessary. No costumes or scripts required.

Second, your fantasies are probably pretty typical. Lehmiller's study revealed there are seven major categories that people fantasize about most. I've dedicated entire chapters to the first two (which are the next lessons in this book!) because they've come up the most frequently as concerns with clients I've worked with and are commonly the subject of DMs and emails I get from women. As such, I'm not going to spend too much time on them in this

lesson. For the remaining five, I'm going to give you examples
I mined from my Shameless clients' 27 Things lists so you can
appreciate the ways in which these fantasies manifest. For each of
these categories, I encourage you to pause and take some notes.
Ask yourself: Have I ever fantasized about this? Do I fantasize
about it often? What does it look like when I do?

1. Multipartner sex (see Lesson 25)
2. Power, control, and rough sex (see Lesson 24)
3. Novelty, adventure, and variety
   This flavor of fantasy is broken down into three smaller
   subcategories:
   - Sexual activities you haven't done before or want to try
     in a new way (e.g., "Masturbate in front of each other,"
     "Double penetration," "Having my partner use a sex toy
     on me in a way that actually feels good")
   - Sex in unique settings (e.g., "Have sex in a hot tub,"
     "Have sex in a dungeon," "Go skinny-dipping in a lake")
   - Unexpected, surprising, or thrilling sexual encounters
     (e.g., "Sensual food and wine exploration while blind-
     folded," "I want to sit on his lap in a short skirt and sexy
     top and have him play with me while he is on a business
     call," "Wear a remote-controlled toy in public")
4. Taboo and forbidden sex (e.g., "Have an affair or one-night
   stand," "Play with knives in the bedroom," "Gag my partner")
5. Swinging, partner sharing, and polyamory (e.g., "Go to a sex
   party and watch my partner with another woman," "I want
   to play together with friends and romantic partners," "Have
   sex with another couple")

6. Intimacy, romance, and passion (e.g., "My partner exploring my body with curiosity," "I want to let go with abandon
   and feel wildly desired," "Have tender, intimate, personal,
   emotional sex with eye contact")
7. Homoeroticism and gender-bending (e.g., "I want a sexual
   experience with another female, no boyfriend, husband,
   etc. involved," "Peg a guy," "I want to play around with my
   masculine side")

As a reminder from when we discussed porn, there's a distinction between a fantasy and a wish. A fantasy is something you think
about that turns you on sexually; a wish is a fantasy you actually
want to enact. What you've read above from Shameless clients are
wishes. These ideas turn them on *and* they're bucket list goals.

But not every fantasy *is* a wish. I once heard a caller on the
Savage Lovecast who could only orgasm if she thought about a
dog fucking her. She was in no way, shape, or form into bestiality.
There was zero chance she ever wanted to do this in real life, but
for whatever reason, it was the image she needed to take her over
the edge to climax.

I say "for whatever reason," because we can never truly know
where our fantasies come from. And trying to suppress them—
which might be your gut instinct when it comes to more taboo
fantasies, like the one above—is actually the worst thing you
can possibly do. As Lehmiller points out, "suppressing thoughts
has the ironic effect of making us *more* likely to think about
them later!"

"All right, Rena. I'm not supposed to suppress them. What do
I do instead?" you might be wondering.

Make friends with them. By now, it'll come as no surprise to you that I'm going to urge you to *get curious* about the fantasy, specifically the underlying emotional need it's meeting.

For example, if the caller I mentioned earlier had come to me with her concerns, I'd probably ask her questions like these:

- What do you imagine is going through the dog's mind as he's penetrating you?
- Is he enjoying it?
- Are you consenting to it, or are you being overpowered?

Maybe she likes the idea of being ravished. Maybe it's the thought of someone (or some*thing*) resorting to its base biological needs and behaving primally. Or maybe it's the fact that the fantasy is itself taboo, and the taboo turns us on like nobody's business.

Depending on the specifics, I'd urge her to find other ways to meet those emotional needs (with a consenting human, of course). Maybe it's through some power play or BDSM. Perhaps pretending to be "hunted" by a partner would scratch the itch. She could also experiment with watching some more obscure fetish porn with a partner. There are many ways to skin this proverbial cat.

I've yet to encounter a client (at least not knowingly) who has fantasies similar to this woman's. I used this as an example of a real fantasy by a real person that most of us would agree we'd never want to enact to show you that pretty much *any* fantasy can be understood if we're willing to get curious about it.

What I do see often, though, are women who are troubled by incest or "rape" fantasies. If you fall into that category, fear not. The next lesson will help!

I mentioned earlier that couples who *enact* their fantasies show the highest rates of relationship satisfaction. Sadly,
Lehmiller's research tells us only 50 percent of folks will ever
disclose their fantasies to their partner because of shame, embar-
rassment, or fear over how their partner will respond.

Yes, fantasies reveal our deepest emotional needs. And that
level of vulnerability can be absolutely terrifying. In addition to
the myriad ways you've already learned to communicate with
your partner (27 Things, "Hey, you know what might be fun to
try?" etc.), I'm going to offer you one more communication tool
that is specific to sexual fantasies.

Each of you will (privately) write down your fantasy on a
piece of paper and then seal it in an envelope. You'll then come
together and—without talking about the fantasy itself—you'll
disclose how you're *feeling* about sharing what's in the envelope. This can look like "I'm super scared about how you'll
react to this. I'm worried you'll think that our sex life isn't good
enough."

From here, keep talking back and forth until both of you feel
safe in sharing and secure that you won't be judged for what's in
the envelope. This conversation may last a while and may not
even conclude in one sitting. Take as long as you each need before
you feel comfortable sharing your fantasies with one another.
Only then will you swap envelopes.

Once you've shared your fantasy with your partner, be prepared to ask (and answer!) the following questions:

- What is it about this fantasy that turns you on?
- How soon do you want to do it?

- If I were to say no to this, would it be a deal breaker?
- Are there some ways we can ease into this fantasy without going all the way the first go-round?

Remember: by making friends with your fantasies, you open up an entire world of exploration, play, and higher relationship satisfaction. Enjoy!

24

Be a Good Girl

So...do you have any kinks?"

My now partner and I sat across from each other at a dimly lit cocktail bar. This was our official first date. I say "official" because although we'd met before and fallen asleep side by side, that had been a chance meeting out in the wild.

I was really proud of myself for asking the question.

I'm so evolved, I thought as I coyly sipped my Naked and Famous, leaving a pregnant pause in the air between us. I expected him to be somehow taken aback, shocked. I expected him to shame me, as I was so used to shaming myself for wanting anything outside the conventional box.

"I have a few," he replied. "Mostly bondage."

"Oh." I hadn't prepared for this. "Like, you like being tied up? Or you like tying other people up?"

"I like tying people up. I like restraining them."

I was curious but couldn't find the words. I was warm in parts of my body that had been cold for a long, long time.

"But you want to know what my biggest kink is?"

I nodded, equally worried that I'd spontaneously combust and that his kink would be so off the grid that I wouldn't be able to wipe the shock off my face.

"What's that?" my voice cracked.

"My kink is finding the thing that's buried so deep inside you that you don't even know what it is...and then giving it to you."

And those were the hottest words anyone had ever said to me.

"How about you?"

I felt like an impostor. Like the nouveau riche kid who's surrounded by high society, nodding along ignorantly to the *New Yorker* references and being asked what the best article I'd recently read was. There was no way I could fake it. I had no experience to draw from.

Unlike what I felt was the majority of the female population, I hadn't read *Fifty Shades of Grey*. I hadn't watched kink-related porn. Other than some teenage experimentation with cheap handcuffs, I couldn't say I'd ever truly done anything kinky before. But I'd seen the movie *Secretary*. *Belle de Jour* is one of my all-time favorite films. Both had turned me on in different and unexpected ways.

"I'm not sure what my kinks are, but I know what I'm curious to try. Bondage, for sure. Surrendering control."

I'd come to find out he knew my type: women who'd been buttoned up and taking charge. Women who were dying to have someone else come in and tell them what to do.

After our next date, I knew we'd have sex.

"So...are you going to tie me up now?" I asked. Somehow wanting to still be in control by knowing what would come next.

And he laughed at me. "No. No. That's not how it works. We're going to ease into this, gently."

We had vanilla sex.

At the time, I would've said "We had great sex." And we did—full of passion and attentiveness.

Looking back and knowing what I now know, I'd say we had vanilla sex. Vanilla in the BDSM way. Vanilla in the sense that it wasn't kinky.

We did ease into it, gently. Just as vanilla sex can become rote and monotonous, so can kinky sex. Over the past five years, he's been mindful to leave surprises to be discovered. To not empty the entire suitcase out on the bed and say, "Here's what I brought for my trip." Instead, our sex life has been an advent calendar that has lasted half a decade.

But what was "the thing"? The thing that was buried so deep inside me that I didn't even know how to name it? The thing that was so uniquely me—not something I saw in a movie or porn—that I needed?

It turned out to be innocence play.

Within the world of BDSM, one person typically assumes the role of dominant and the other submissive (people can also identify as "switch" and vacillate between the two). There are varying levels of dominance and submission, ranging from getting a mere slap on the ass to being told what to eat every meal of the day (and asking your Dom's permission to do so).

One feature of a D/s (Dom/sub) dynamic that's relatively common, though, is how the sub is to refer to the Dom. "Sir" is a common label.

So is "Daddy."

"Don't ever ask me to call you Daddy," I told him in the first few months of our relationship. "It creeps me the fuck out."

Fast-forward two years, to a night we were in bed, feeling the effects of the weed gummies we'd chewed. "Can I call you Daddy?"

That was the thing I wanted. The thing buried so deep inside me that I was revolted at the mere suggestion of it. And perhaps that distaste was itself the surest tell that it was what I wanted. Yet another sign that the taboo is, in fact, what turns us on.

Yes, our biggest sex organ is the one between our ears...blah blah blah. But what was going on between my ears? What was the underlying emotional need I was trying to meet?

I didn't have the answer that night. And I didn't need it. I just knew my erotic imagination had sunk its teeth into something delicious that I didn't want to stop tasting.

But now I've taken it out. I've examined the delicious thing. I've rolled it in my hands with curiosity. And here's what I've discovered about how I enjoy being submissive:

I'm not into pain for the sake of pain.

I like being told what to do and rewarded for it.

I crave the feeling of being nurtured and taken care of.

I like being "taught" about my body.

You may be judging me right now. "Wait, what? A former sex crimes and child abuse prosecutor wants to be treated like she's innocent and fucked by her 'Daddy'?"

The twisted irony of it isn't lost on me.

But look closer at what you've also learned by this point. Are you yucking my yum? Approach your revulsion from a place of curiosity. We don't choose our kinks: they choose us.

There's a slew of emotional needs I'm meeting through this fantasy: I feel held and cared for. I'm rewarded for having a positive relationship with pleasure and my body. I'm encouraged to approach my sexuality from a place of curiosity. The list goes on and on.

The overwhelming majority of women (93 percent!) have fantasized about being sexually dominated. Schoolgirl and babysitter porn—famous for their power dynamics—are ubiquitous to the point of becoming tropes. And once you look at all the evidence spread out before you, the question transforms from "How could this be?" to "How could this *not* be?"

Am I saying that all women in the recesses of their imagination want to engage in some form of age or innocence play? Not at all. But when we're talking about a number as high as 93 percent when it comes to sexual submission fantasies, we're looking at a massive elephant in the room.

Fifty Shades of Grey sold more copies than *any other book in the last decade*. Read. That. Again.

That book stirred something in the female consciousness. At a point in human history when we're expected to make more decisions than ever—as partners, mothers, bosses—is it any wonder we have a seemingly universal emotional need for someone else to take the reins? Doesn't it make sense that we want to *just be*?

If my clients are any indication, the answer is a huge, resounding "Fuck yes."

I could write an entire book composed of their submission fantasies. Of the shock they emit as we pore over their BDSM test results and the eventual realization that it all makes sense for them too. Of the commonalities I see in their erotic short stories:

of strangers filled with intense passion and desire for them, being skillfully ravaged, surrendering control, just being.

I've also talked clients through incest fantasies. "I don't actually want to have sex with my [brother, father, uncle]. What the fuck is wrong with me?"

And then we dive deeper. Typically these are D/s fantasies wrapped up and tied with a big taboo ribbon. They meet the emotional needs of surrendering control while also giving us that sense of erotic transgression. Not all our fantasies are wishes, remember?

So let's talk about "rape" fantasies too. I use quotes around the word "rape" because we're not actually talking about rape. When we're walking down a dark alleyway at night, are we actually secretly wishing someone would jump out and violently assault us? No. Just like we don't literally want to have sex with a family member, we don't literally want to be raped. Yet nearly two-thirds of women have had "forced seduction" or "consensual non-consent" fantasies. So yes. This is a common fantasy. But it's also one of the most troubling, especially for survivors of sexual trauma.

My client Becca had spent nearly a decade in a controlling relationship where sex was rarely consensual. "And now when I masturbate, I think about him raping me. It's the only thing that can bring me over the edge to orgasm."

She was shaming herself for staying in the relationship as long as she had, then compounding the shame by deriving pleasure from recalling the abuse.

"Do you actually want to have sex with him again?" I asked.

"Hell no! The thought of even seeing him again makes me sick. He destroyed me."

"So this is a fantasy, but it isn't a wish." I described the distinctions and reminded her that our fantasies shed a light on our emotional needs. "What do you think those needs are, Becca?"

"I want to feel like I've made sense of all of it. That maybe it couldn't have been all bad, and that's why I stayed as long as I did. But maybe it's more than that. Maybe it's that I wanted it to have been my choice."

And there, my friends, is the distinction.

In an actual sexual assault, we don't have a choice. But in our erotic imagination, *we do*. We're orchestrating the scene. Dan Savage often refers to BDSM as a naked, grown-up version of cops and robbers, which is a reminder that we are engaging in pretend. In play.

In consensual D/s play, the submissive is choosing to give up control. But after the scene ends, the sub gets the control back. In Becca's relationship, there was no "end scene," no director to yell "cut." This wasn't cops and robbers; this was the equivalent of literally being held hostage at gunpoint during a bank robbery. In her fantasy, though, she could reclaim that control.

For some women, wanting to be subjugated at all is troubling. If we set aside incest, forced seduction, and age-play fantasies, just the idea of *wanting* to be dominated can cause us to question our identity as strong women.

I'm here to tell you that wherever you fall on this spectrum, there isn't a single thing wrong with you. You aren't less of an empowered woman or a feminist. In fact, it's probably *because* you are empowered in your daily life that your imagination is craving something where you're choosing to relinquish that power.

"But, Rena. That doesn't describe me."

It may genuinely not. As someone who felt the shame of her fantasies, the last thing I'd want to do is shame you for the fantasies you *don't* have.

So say you're in the 7 percent of women who haven't had submission fantasies. Chances are still fairly high you know someone who has. And in the spirit of not yucking anyone's yum, I'd encourage you to use the knowledge in this chapter as power. To be the person who tries to understand. To champion curiosity.

So let's get curious.

You may already have an idea of what you're into (or not into) when it comes to kink. Or you may be firmly convinced you're vanilla (remember: that doesn't mean boring!) through and through.

Regardless, I'm going to encourage you to take the BDSM test that, at the time of this writing, is the most widely used questionnaire to show you where your kinky preferences are.

One thing to keep in mind before you start: there may be some questions on there that shock you. "Wait—that's a thing?!" Yes. That's a thing. It may not be *your* thing. You made a promise to not yuck anyone's yum. Honor that commitment by filling out the questionnaire from a place of curiosity, not judgment!

Head on over to bdsmtest.org and take the test. You'll then get your results in a percentage format, starting with desires that are most appealing to you. Within the test is a glossary of sorts to define the terms you'll see on your results.

Here's what I want you to pay special attention to: your top three results and where vanilla "lives" on your list (and how far it is from the next result).

So for example, say vanilla is at the top of your list, coming in at 93 percent. But let's say rope bunny (a.k.a. someone who likes to be tied up) came in at 89 percent, and voyeur came in at 87 percent. What that says to me is that you don't *need* kink in order for you to have a sexually fulfilling sex life. The kink is the cherry on top of your vanilla sundae. You'd like to be tied up here and there. And maybe it'd be fun to watch some porn (or even attend a sex party) with a partner. But the full range of your sexual expression doesn't depend on it.

But let's say vanilla is hovering somewhere in the 50 percent to 60 percent range, as is common with many of the clients I've worked with, a lot of whom have never dabbled in kink before. This is a sign you're missing out on the kind of sex you actually crave.

Does this mean you need to stop what you're doing and start building a sex dungeon? No. Obviously what lives *above* the vanilla on your BDSM results is going to vary from person to person. There isn't a one-size-fits-all prescription I can give you to start you on your kink journey. The "primal" person is looking for something different from the "sadist" and so forth.

What I would encourage you to do, though, is explore further. Take the terms that rank high on your list and use them to search for porn. See what resonates with you and what doesn't.

If you're partnered, ask your partner to take the test too. And then share your results with each other at the same time. (The last thing we want is for one person to consciously or subconsciously respond in a way to align with their partner.) Approach the results from a place of curiosity and ask, "How can we start playing with these?" As you know by now having read this far in the book, baby steps are key. If you discover you're into receiving pain (a masochist), don't try nipple clamps if you've never even experienced having your nipples pinched before (trust me on this one).

Have a *very* clear safe word. "No" happens to be the shittiest safe word of all time, especially if you're role-playing. It doesn't need to be as outlandish as "pink rhinoceros" either. My partner and I have literally used the term "safe word" as our safe word for years.

I know I said there isn't a one-size-fits-all prescription, but there's something close to it: a sleep mask. Yes, the kind you'd use to keep the light out. By restricting one of your five senses (your sense of sight), you can gently ease into experimenting with power dynamics and surrendering control. Each of you can take turns wearing the mask. Do you like being the one in control or the one surrendering? Do you find it easier to incorporate a bit of role-play and assume character without the insecurities that come along with your partner looking you straight in the eye?

As you explore, know that your BDSM results aren't set in stone. Our fantasies are a glimpse into our emotional needs, a snapshot of who we are at a given point in time. And those needs are constantly fluctuating. This isn't like your astrological chart. I'm a Scorpio sun, Aquarius moon, Aquarius rising. My BDSM results change every year I take the test. I've had "vanilla" clients return to me a year later, surprised at how kinky their test results have become. I've seen self-proclaimed kinky women realize they want to take a break from it. Change is not only allowed, it's encouraged.

Whether you choose to incorporate whips and chains or lean into some gentle psychological power exchange, remember: BDSM is a type of role-play. And you can't spell role-play without play!

25

Make It a Group Thing

My partner and I were at Lovely Fate, my favorite play party in LA. I love hanging on the party's back patio: meeting couples and learning their origin stories. Getting into deep conversations with professional dominants about the power of BDSM as a tool in trauma healing. Whipping out the notes app on my phone to jot down recommendations for places to check out during upcoming trips we have planned.

These are my people.

But once we go upstairs—past the public flogging on a Saint Andrew's cross and the crowd gathering around a woman riding a Sybian in the lounge—everyone else disappears. The people fucking around us cease to exist. The performative grunts and groans become ambient noise. In those moments, it's just me and him. Considering how much I love porn, I was shocked to learn that I'm not really a voyeur when it comes to public sex.

Tonight was different. It was the first time we'd brought a

woman we were dating to a party with us. It hadn't dawned on me that having another person there would disrupt our well-worn public sex groove. But as my partner was inside me and she explored my body with her hands and mouth, the scene came to a screeching halt.

"Oh my god. Anthony?!" she squealed, popping up and running toward a guy standing in the room's doorway. This would've been normal at a bar or brunch or Disneyland or pretty much anywhere else in the world that wasn't a play party.

"Looks like she saw a friend," my partner said as we both covered our mouths, laughing. "Let's keep going without her."

Yes, tonight was different. But also, *she* was different: she was the first woman we'd ventured out into the world with as our third. Dinner. Drinks. We'd gone out to a dance club together a few weeks beforehand. Three adults having a blast on the dance floor, giggling while we took turns making out. Him teasing me the next day for how excited and giddy I'd been the whole night, "like a fucking schoolgirl."

We hadn't been allowed to do this before. And I don't mean that in some sort of existential way. When we'd previously dated women, the entire world was closed down because of the pandemic. There were no first dates out in the wild.

At that time, we'd set up a couples profile on Feeld, open about our D/s dynamic and shared love of drinking whiskey and playing stoned Scrabble. I handled our DMs on the account, and if there was someone we felt we vibed with, we'd schedule a Zoom call to chat further (thanks, pandemic!).

If that went well, the three of us would hop on a group text thread to get to know each other better. The usual stuff like favorite bands, movies, books. And the more explicit, like hard limits and sexual fantasies.

The first woman we met in person was a sweet submissive who loved cats and video games. She was already in a primary relationship with a loving partner who had moved to a different part of the state to get a PhD. Her partner wasn't kinky and encouraged her to indulge in her submission fantasies outside the relationship.

We'd spent a good hour or so chatting at my partner's place. Again, about the usual stuff and also the more explicit. And as she sat crisscross on my man's living room floor—a slice of leftover Thanksgiving pecan pie beside her, cards from a game we'd played still strewn on the rug—the panic set in.

"Can I have a word with you outside?" I asked him. On the deck, I hugged myself for warmth. "I don't know if I can do this," I admitted.

"Okay. Like, you want to call the whole thing off, or...?"

"No. No. It's not that. I just can't watch you seduce her. Like, can we just teleport into the bedroom and get this whole thing started already? I don't think I'll be able to handle watching you make the move on her."

You see, all my fantasies of seeing him with another woman started once they were midscene, in the act. I hadn't once stopped to consider what the opening sequence would look like. I wanted this to feel arousing, like we were starring in our own porn. And the story I was telling myself was that my partner's act of seduction turned this into a steamy romance film instead. And what happens in romance films? People fall in love. And what is the feeling of being scared that your partner might fall in love with another person called? Yep, jealousy.

But he didn't question my why at the time. We agreed I'd go into the bathroom and that by the time I came out, they would have already kissed. And then it would be my turn.

And, for a few years, this was pretty much how our first time went down with every single woman we ended up having a three-some with. I know that (most) porn isn't real life, and real life isn't porn. But this is a small concession we've all made so that I'd feel safe in the moment.

"Hey, you two, I'm going to the bathroom. Get up to whatever you want to get up to!" had been my awkward green light to the other parties. And what has happened after has varied. We've had marathon all-nighters, exhausting entire boxes of condoms, that picked back up again after breakfast. We've acted out entire scripted role-play scenes, then parted ways before 11:00 p.m. We've had nights of cuddle puddles and three-way pillow talk, our bodies still sticky with sweat.

No two people are alike. No two threesomes are ever the same. I learn more about myself—my likes and dislikes, my triggers and fantasies—from every single experience we've had. I've also grown closer to my partner with every single group encounter. There are horror stories out there, to be sure. But people fantasize about multiple partner experiences more than any other fantasy. (Only 5 percent of men and 13 percent of women have *never* fantasized about it.) And with numbers that high, it's time to have an honest conversation about how to move past our fears and begin safely indulging in our desires.

I'll start by admitting I have no experience with being with more than one man or full swaps with heterosexual couples. My experience until now is limited to threesomes with a male and a female (MFF) or with two females (FFF). Through this lesson, though, I hope to give you some basic groundwork to set you up for success, regardless of the configuration you're fantasizing about.

If you've had multiple partner fantasies, you're in the overwhelming majority, yes. But as you've now learned, not all fantasies are wishes. If you know right off the bat you don't actually want to have group sex, cool. Keep thinking about it while you masturbate. Keep watching the orgy or threesome porn that fuels your erotic imagination. Or attend a sex party but keep your hands to yourself.

You can also explore meeting your fantasy's underlying emotional need without bringing other people into the bedroom. Say you get off on the idea of being the center of attention, a group of hungry hands groping your body. You can wear a blindfold and use your imagination while your partner touches you. Say you have a specific woman in mind who you'd like to bring into the fold. You can experiment with some light role-play and pretend to be that other person.

But say you want to take it to the next level. You've got the blueprint for the house. You have a vision of what the completed project will look like. How, then, do you begin to lay a solid foundation for it?

Trust is the bedrock. You can't build a house on shaky ground. You can't have a successful group romp if you don't fully trust all the players. Don't expect a positive outcome from a threesome if your relationship is already on the fritz. Sure, it *can* happen. Just like having a baby *can* save your relationship. But the odds are stacked against you.

Note that I'm not talking about opening up the relationship so you can each date or sleep with other people. I've actually seen this save relationships that have fizzled or situations where partners have misaligned libidos or kinks. I discussed ENM at length back in Lesson 14, "Examine Your Default Setting," in case you're looking for a refresher!

But if you're wanting to explore with your current partner, threesomes and group sex are another type of ENM and can peacefully coexist with other styles. They can also be a way to *start* opening up your relationship. If your partner can see with their own eyes that sleeping with another person isn't going to drop a bomb in your relationship, this can foster a greater level of trust in what you'll do when you're playing or dating solo.

I worked with a client, Marisol, who I'll talk about by way of illustration.

Marisol and her husband had been married for eighteen years and have two kids. She came to me on the heels of asking him for a divorce.

"I want more," she told me during our consultation. "I've lost sight of who I am. I want adventure and joy and for life not to feel forced."

For nearly fifteen years, she'd questioned whether she was actually wired for monogamy. But she'd kept that to herself, instead playing the dutiful role of wife and mother.

"I want forward movement," she told me. She was still in love with her husband but couldn't fathom a scenario where she'd be able to inject adventure back into the marriage and indulge her sexual curiosities.

"Let's see what we can do," I told her.

She had an honest discussion with her husband about opening up. They agreed to start a Feeld account and eventually began chatting with other couples. In the meantime, they invested in improving their own sex life through activities like practicing sensate focus, buying toys, and using the Paired app on a daily basis. After a while on their Feeld account, they met one couple in particular who loved being watched and listened to while having sex. The four of them would get on video chat, Marisol and her husband listening intently. And it changed everything for them.

"We're having the kind of sex I actually crave. I don't feel trapped, suffocated, or controlled anymore. This hasn't just saved our marriage," she told me. "It's strengthened it."

Throughout the time I worked with Marisol, she and her husband had solidified their foundation. Now they were ready to build on it.

Much to my absolute fucking delight, I got this message from her a few months later:

> OMG we had the best experience last night. The couple was from Feeld. We had sex under Christmas lights and next to the Christmas tree after an amazing home cooked meal/drinks and two hours of laughter and conversation. Best way to have a first experience together. It was the hottest thing I've ever done in my life. [My husband] and I are feeling so good. We went to breakfast today and have had sex twice since.

They'd done everything right. She was honest with him about needing to open up to stay in the marriage. He was responsive to her. They worked on expanding their own communication and strengthening their connection. Then and only then did they start dipping their toes into the idea of group play, first through listening to another couple fuck, then ultimately building trust with a pair they ended up having their first foursome with. From there, they each began exploring on Feeld solo, going out on dates with others.

This book has given you tools to build a solid relationship foundation, in and out of the bedroom. (It's also taught you the important of being fuck yes about your relationship and what to do if you aren't!) If you want to start building on that foundation in the form of a threesome, foursome, or moresome, keep these pointers in mind.

Take Baby Steps

"God, Rena and her baby steps." Yes. You're probably sick of the term by now.

But baby steps are critical regardless of how solid your foundation is. Before my partner and I had our first threesome, I'd fantasized a lot about watching him fuck another woman. It turned me on to no end. If the idea itself fills you with horror and anxiety, *don't do it*.

But if the thought does excite you, start gently leaning into it. Watch some porn together, and notice how you react. Does seeing your partner get turned on by someone on the screen make you insanely jealous? Better to know you're threatened by watching an actor before bringing a 3D human being into the mix.

The day before our first threesome, I got my period. Although my partner and I were used to shower sex and laying down towels, the thought of bringing in a third party for the first time while on my cycle didn't appeal to me. So I suggested ahead of time we take anything below our (her and my) belts off the table the first time around, "to make it fair." She was completely on board. Down to our panties, she and I explored each other's bodies. The threesome ended with both of us going down on my partner and feeling safe that we could move on to penetration and oral on each other the next time we saw each other (which we did).

While my period was initially an unwelcome and frustrating surprise, it ended up being the one thing that paced us the first time around. I'm not suggesting you have to plan a threesome around your menstrual cycle (if you have one). There are plenty of other ways to take baby steps. You can all meet somewhere public the first time and agree not to go back to anyone's house after. You can plan to stay fully clothed and limit yourselves to making out and some petting (very junior high, I know). You can take oral sex or penetration off the table the first time. Not only does the baby steps approach allow you to gauge your jealousy and comfort level in increments, it builds sexual anticipation (which we know is a good thing!).

Search Responsibly

While on a trip with some female friends to the central coast, I got into a conversation with a man and woman at a bar. They claimed to be "just friends" and explained they'd come out to grab some drinks while their respective spouses were at home watching the kids.

"We've known each other forever. We're like brother and

sister!" they assured me. They were well dressed with college educations and respectable careers that they talked about at length. I had no reason to doubt them or think they wanted anything but conversation from me.

Fast-forward to the three of us in an upscale hotel room up the street that the dude rented as an excuse to all keep hanging out after the bar closed.

"Our kids are sleeping at our houses, so we can't go there" was their only explanation.

I was definitely attracted to her but didn't want anything to do with him. She and I played together on the condition—*my* condition—he stay in the corner of the room and keep his hands off me.

I woke up the next morning completely alone. My phone, wallet, and kidneys were intact (thank god). I had no clue who these people really were—no last names, no cell phone numbers exchanged—but I absolutely knew that their claim to be "like brother and sister!" didn't align to what happened once we got behind closed doors.

This was definitely *not* a shining moment for me. I felt used. I felt lied to. I woke up in a situation that could have gone much, much worse, but it was still incredibly shitty. Don't be those people. Don't treat single folks like prey or currency and manipulate them. Just...don't.

Be decent. Be respectful. Be honest about what you're looking for.

If you know you'd like to hook up with a couple, try going to a play party first. Kasidie.com is a great social media site for "lifestyle" events geared toward swingers. If you lean kinky, check out FetLife for events in your city. Reddit can also be a good spot for searching for groups and networks close to home.

If you're on the hunt for something more private (i.e., not a play party), Feeld is your best bet. You'll find singles and partners looking to explore. But for the love of god, be direct in your profile, and read other people's profiles too. When I was running our joint account on Feeld, I was bombarded with couples looking for foursomes despite very clearly stating we were not. Be true to your word, and take others at theirs. If you're looking for a femme submissive (as we were), say it. If you're looking for a one time thing, say it. If you're looking to form a bond with a couple and (ideally) become consistent play partners, say it.

Which brings me to my next point.

Communicate

Communicate. Every. Step. Of. The. Way.

Once you've found the person (or persons) you want to bring into your bedroom, set up your expectations.

WHAT ARE OUR RULES AROUND USING PROTECTION?

For example, my partner always uses a condom with another player. We don't use one together, even if we're joined by a third party. Yes, this isn't the most eco-friendly way of doing things (lots of condoms tossed in the trash, then replaced by fresh ones), but it's what we've all been on board with at this point. Sharing STI results is also pretty common before group play. Some people may also only want to use their own toys.

WHAT ARE YOU *INTO*?

Do you want to be fucked by another man as your partner watches in the corner? Say that. Do you want to be tied up while a couple has their way with you? Say that. Can you only orgasm through oral? Say that.

IS THERE ANYTHING THAT'S OFF-LIMITS OR THAT YOU'RE *NOT* INTO?

This is especially important if you start leaning into kink territory. Don't make any assumptions that just because someone is kinky, you're allowed to bring out the whips and chains. Also, be sure to ask about preferred terms (Daddy, Sir, Mommy, Mistress) that you all agree to beforehand. Similarly, find out if there are any words you don't like in the bedroom. I've been with women who like being degraded—being called sluts and whores—and women who firmly don't. You may also find some people don't want certain types of play (anal is a common example).

WHAT'S OUR SAFE WORD?

You still need one, even if you're not getting kinky. It's important that if one person in the group wants to pull the rip cord, the rest of you will be cool with it. Consent is sexy. I dub myself "the consent fairy" during group play because I check in all the damn time with everyone involved. Know what else is sexy? All parties knowing they're free to revoke consent at any time. I talked about safe words in the last lesson, but in the context of vanilla sex, something as simple as "Hey, I want to take a break" or "I'm not super into this" is your signal to stop.

WHAT'S OUR EXPECTATION *AFTER*?

My partner and I make it clear to our play partners that they're welcome to stay the night but are under no pressure whatsoever to do so. Some have. Others haven't. Some have preemptively said, "I'll probably head home to my own bed later," and some have said, "Good to know! I'll play it by ear." If you know you have a preference one way or the other, say it.

You know the golden rule? Treating others how you would want to be treated? Bring that into the bedroom with you, regardless of how many people you're joined by! Be honest with each other. Be good *to* each other!

Conclusion: Your Happy Ending

am so proud of you!

You did it. You made it to the end of the book.

By now, you've (hopefully!) amassed a tool kit to get you started on your shameless journey to deep intimacy, honest pleasure, and a life you love. You have mindset practices you can use to get clear on your desires and lower the volume on your shame tape. You've harnessed your 80-year-old badass and started examining your current (and future) relationships to see if you're settling for less than you deserve. You've gotten your cool girl act in check and have lots of tools to explore and talk about what you want in and out of the bedroom.

But most importantly: you've taken a hard look at how you live and love from a place of curiosity instead of judgment. You've upped your own yum factor and know not to yuck anyone else's. And you've read the stories of real, breathing women who've walked a similar path.

Here's the part where I'm supposed to neatly package everything you've learned, tie it up with a profound ribbon, and present it to you like a pretty gift.

But I'm not going to.

Because intimacy, sex, and relationships are anything but polished. Life is beautiful because it's messy and imperfect.

I'd be lying if I said I'd tried everything at this point. I'd be grossly exaggerating if I claimed I had it all figured out. I would be absolutely full of shit if I made lofty assertions about you being "healed." But I know I'm leaving you in the most capable hands—your own.

By the time you read this, I'll probably have another book's worth of anecdotes and lessons I've learned. Because life is meant to be the journey. And I hope this book is the beginning—not the end—of yours.

Acknowledgments

Think writing a book is difficult? Thanking the people who made a book possible is even harder. Gulp.

To my partner, Dan: so many of the experiences discussed in these pages wouldn't have been possible had you not been by my side the last five-plus years. Thank you for seeing me for who I am, opening me up to a world of love and erotic exploration, and allowing me to share these experiences with readers. That last one is particularly massive, given how private you are. Your willingness to pull back the curtain on our intimate lives is the most generous gift I've ever received. I love you beyond words.

A huge thanks to my friend and author Chad Kultgen. You asked me over a vegan dinner two years ago why the hell I hadn't started writing a book already. That single question ended up being the proverbial match that lit a fire under my ass to actually do it.

Thank you to Jennifer Dickinson, my friend and writing coach, for guiding me through what ended up being several completed chapters of this book. You told me I was a beautiful writer, then vigorously challenged me. This final product wouldn't be here had you not given me equal measures of both.

To Deanna Moffitt for generously reading the introductory

chapters of this book and giving valuable feedback. But so many more thanks because you were the first coach I ever hired. You are the person who said, "You know you can just buy your own damned insurance," when I had every reason to believe I couldn't unlock the golden handcuffs that kept me shackled to a government job. This book certainly wouldn't have been possible had you not pushed me to see life beyond a nine to five.

A massive thanks to Camille Saltzman, one of my first Shameless clients and an early reader. You've been by my side through every single painstaking milestone in the book's progress and are one of the dearest friends I've ever had. I don't even want to think about what my life would look like without you in it, so I'm not gonna.

Thank you to Hilary Swanson and Julia Pastore. Your editorial guidance was instrumental in having a pitchable book proposal that would appeal to publishers.

To John "The Angry Therapist" Kim. You've championed me since my early days of coach training and opened doors I never could have imagined, the largest being your generous introduction to my literary agent, Laura. I will never stop being grateful for your mentorship.

To Laura Yorke, my self-proclaimed "book yenta": I literally threw my phone on a sidewalk after pilates when I saw your email asking to set up a call to discuss representation. On that call, you said you'd always fight for me but never bullshit me, which resonated deeply with my inner lawyer. I know you're selective as hell when it comes to taking on clients (and I'm still not sure why you chose me!) but picking you as my agent was a no-brainer. Thank you for believing in this project and in me.

Speaking of believing in this project: I knew very little about how publishing works when I decided to write a book. And now that I do, I'm blown away that Sourcebooks took a chance on a first-time non-fiction author without a PhD after her name. Thank you to my editor Findlay McCarthy for bringing this book into the Sourcebooks family, giving me major artistic liberty (a decision I hope you won't regret!), and responding to every anxiety-induced text with your signature blend of humor, love, and expressive emoji.

Thank you to Sourcebooks editor Liv Turner for taking on the monumental task of bringing this project from manuscript to book. You made the editorial transition seamless and your out-of-the-box thinking has been a god-send to such an unconventional project.

Most families would be horrified to know their daughter or sister would be publishing a memoir-driven sexual self-help book, but mine have been huge supporters every step of the way. I hope your enthusiasm persists after you read this book. (Or even if you don't. Yeah, you may not want to read this book.) I love you all so much.

Thank you to my colleague, friend, and author Dr. MaryCatherine "MC" McDonald for double-checking my discussion of trauma for accuracy.

Another huge thanks to writer and activist Jaclyn Moore for sensitivity-checking how trans bodies and sex are talked about in this book.

Last, to every Shameless woman I've had the honor of working with: YOU are the reason this book exists. Your stories. Your strength. Your vulnerability. Your trust in me and the process. Your unwavering commitment to reclaiming "Shameless" as a badge of honor. You are the most incredible women I've ever known.

Notes

Introduction

96 percent of women: Justin J. Lehmiller, *Tell Me What You Want: The Science of Sexual Desire and How It Can Improve Your Sex Life* (New York: Hachette Go, 2018), 19.

more women are cheating: Wednesday Martin, *Untrue: Why Nearly Everything We Believe About Women, Lust, and Infidelity Is Wrong and How the New Science Can Set Us Free* (New York: Little, Brown Spark 2018), 4.

Lesson 7: Love Your Body with the Lights On

Within a three-year period: Erica Goode, "Study Finds TV Alters Fiji Girls' View of Body," *New York Times*, May 20, 1999, https://www.nytimes.com/1999/05/20/world/study-finds-tv-alters-fiji-girls-view-of-body.html.

Lesson 8: Turn Yourself On

sexual pioneers William Masters: Sexual Medical Society of North America, "What Is Sensate Focus and How Does It Work?," SMSNA For Patients, accessed March 18, 2023, https://www.smsna.org/patients/did-you-know/what-is-sensate-focus-and-how-does-it-work.

Lesson 10: Find Your People

"If we can share": Brené Brown, *Daring Greatly: How the Courage to Be Vulnerable Transforms the Way We Live, Love, Parent, and Lead* (New York: Avery, 2015), 75.

Lesson 11: If It's Not a Fuck Yes, It's a No

"In a world where": Esther Perel, *The State of Affairs: Rethinking Infidelity* (New York: Harper, 2017), 50.

"Like milk, your relationship": John Kim, "6 Steps to Bounce Back From an Expired Relationship," *Psychology Today*, December 21, 2016, https://www.psychologytoday.com/us/blog/the-angry-therapist/201612/6-steps-bounce-back-expired-relationship.

Lesson 12: Do It Soon

"It's always amazed me": Dan Savage, *Savage Love from A to Z: Advice on Sex and Relationships, Dating and Mating, Exes and Extras* (Seattle: Sasquatch Books, 2021), 19.

Lesson 13: Stop Playing the Cool Girl

"Staying vulnerable is a risk": Brené Brown, *The Gifts of Imperfection* (Center City, MN: Hazelden Publishing, 2022), 71.

Lesson 14: Examine Your Default Setting

"statistics range from as low": Martin, *Untrue*, 4.

"95% of respondents": Martin, *Untrue*, 23.

Rates of jealousy aren't: Terri D. Conley, Any C. Moors, Jes L. Matsick, and Ali Ziegler, "The Fewer the Merrier? Assessing Stigma Surrounding Consensually Non-Monogamous Romantic Relationships," *Analyses of Social Issues and Public Policy* 13, no. 1 (December 2013): 1–30, https://doi.org/10.1111/j.1530-2415.2012.01286.x.

Lesson 15: Go with the Flow

"safe space for bisexual": "Welcome to Skirt Club," Skirt Club, accessed March 19, 2023, www.skirtclub.co.uk/home.

Lesbian and queer bars: Sarah Marloff, "The Rise and Fall of America's Lesbian Bars," *Smithsonian Magazine*, January 21, 2021, https://www.smithsonianmag.com/travel/rise-and-fall-americas-lesbian-bars-180976801/.

two new ones have opened: Tejal Rao, "The Lesbian Bar Isn't Dead. It's Pouring Orange Wine in Los Angeles." *New York Times*, April 1, 2023, https://www.nytimes.com/2023/04/01/dining/drinks/lesbian-bars-los-angeles.html.

In 2019, only 65 percent: Jessica Klein, "Why More Women Identify as Sexually

Fluid Than Men," *Lovelife* (blog), BBC, June 15, 2021, https://www.bbc .com/worklife/article/20210610-why-more-women-identify-as-sexually -fluid-than-men.

Feeld was originally called: Wikipedia, s.v. "Feeld," last modified April 6, 2023, https://en.wikipedia.org/wiki/Feeld.

"women have more orgasms": Laurie Mintz, *Becoming Cliterate: Why Orgasm Equality Matters—And How to Get It* (New York: HarperOne, 2017), 141.

Lesson 16: Get Creative

"When we are no longer": Viktor E. Frankl, *Man's Search for Meaning* (Boston: Beacon Press, 2006), 135.

Lesson 17: Give it Room to Breathe

"Fire needs air": Esther Perel, "The Secret to Desire in a Long-Term Relationship," TED, February 14, 2013, accessed April 12, 2023, https://www.ted.com /talks/esther_perel_the_secret_to_desire_in_a_long_term_relationship /comments/transcript.

Lesson 19: Talk about It

50 percent of women who discuss: John M. Gottman, *The Science of Trust: Emotional Attunement for Couples* (New York: W. W. Norton, 2011), 264.

Esther Perel recommends couples: Esther Perel, "Bringing Home the Erotic: 5 Ways to Create Meaningful Connections with Your Partner," *Esther Perel* (blog), accessed March 15, 2023, https://www.estherperel.com /blog/5-ways-to-create-meaningful-connections.

Lesson 20: Schedule It

Only 15 percent of women: Emily Nagoski, *Come as You Are: The Surprising New Science That Will Transform Your Sex Life* (New York: Simon & Schuster, 2015), 225.

"Think of a positive": Nagoski, *Come as You Are*, 95.

"think of a not-so-great": Nagoski, *Come as You Are*, 101.

Lesson 21: Make Porn Your Friend

"Bellesa Films captures real": "Bellesa Films," accessed November 18, 2019, https://www.bellesa.co/assets/files/bellesa-films.pdf.

"#realworld people—singles, couples": "Our House, Our Rules," MakeLoveNotPorn, accessed April 12, 2023, https://makelovenotporn.tv/our -house-our-rules.

"a creator-centered platform": "About Us," Lustery, accessed February 21, 2023, https://lustery.com/about.

"LGBTQ+ adult film performers": "About CrashPadSeries," CrashPadSeries, accessed April 12, 2023, https://crashpadseries.com/queer-porn/crash padseries/.

"BDSM is about respect": "About Us," Kink, accessed November 3, 2022, https://www.kink.com/page/about-us.

"We are as obsessive": "About," Dipsea, accessed March 14, 2023, https://www.dipseastories.com/about/.

women who watch it: Sean M. McNabney, Krisztina Hevesi, and David L. Rowland, "Effects of Pornography Use and Demographic Parameters on Sexual Response during Masturbation and Partnered Sex in Women," *International Journal of Environmental Research and Public Health* 17, no. 9 (April 2020): 3130, https://doi.org/10.3390/ijerph17093130.

A 2018 study by Pornhub: "Women of the World," Pornhub, March 8, 2019, https://www.pornhub.com/insights/women-of-the-world.

Lesson 22: Bring in the Toys

as it doesn't for roughly: Mintz, *Becoming Cliterate*, 14.

So they're still getting: Mintz, *Becoming Cliterate*, 73.

Lesson 23: Use Your Imagination

"sexual fantasies reveal our": Perel, "Bringing Home the Erotic."

Research by Justin J. Lehmiller : Lehmiller, *Tell Me What You Want*, 165.

"A sexual fantasy is": Lehmiller, *Tell Me What You Want*, 2.

"suppressing thoughts has the": Lehmiller, *Tell Me What You Want*, 3.

Lesson 24: Be a Good Girl

The overwhelming majority of women: Justin Lehmiller, "3 Sex Fantasies That Are More Common Than You Think," Sex & Psychology by Dr. Justin Lehmiller, February , 2019, https://www.sexandpsychology.com/blog/2019/2/1 /three-sexual-fantasies-that-are-more-common-than-you-think-2/.

Fifty Shades of Grey **sold:** "'Fifty Shades of Grey' Was the Best-Selling Book of the Decade in the U.S., The NPD Group Says," NPD, December 18, 2019, https://www.npd.com/news/press-releases/2019/fifty-shades-of -grey-was-the-best-selling-book-of-the-decade-in-the-u-s-the-npd -group-says/.

Yet nearly two-thirds: Lehmiller, *Tell Me What You Want*, 27.

Lesson 25: Make It a Group Thing

But people fantasize about multiple partner: Lehmiller, *Tell Me What You Want*, 14.

About the Author

© Daniel Bergeron

Rena Martine is a former sex crimes prosecutor turned women's intimacy expert known for her infectious energy, refreshing candor, and straightforward approach. She's impacted thousands of women globally as a certified coach, educator, and speaker with a mission to reclaim the term "Shameless" as a badge of honor. A native Angeleno, Rena calls Echo Park home and happily lives around the corner from her partner. When she's not chasing her Siamese cat Chooch around, you can find her connecting with people she loves most, with a smile on her face and (sometimes!) a bourbon cocktail in her hand.